An R Companion for the Third Edition of The Fundamentals of Political Science Research

An R Companion for the Third Edition of The Fundamentals of Political Science Research offers students a chance to delve into the world of R using real political data sets and statistical analysis techniques directly from Paul M. Kellstedt and Guy D. Whitten's best-selling textbook. Built in parallel with the main text, this workbook teaches students to apply the techniques they learn in each chapter by reproducing the analyses and results from each lesson using R. Students will also learn to create all of the tables and figures found in the textbook, leading to an even greater mastery of the core material. This accessible, informative, and engaging companion walks through the use of R step-by-step, using command lines and screenshots to demonstrate proper use of the software. With the help of these guides, students will become comfortable creating, editing, and using data sets in R to produce original statistical analyses for evaluating causal claims. End-of-chapter exercises encourage this innovation by asking students to formulate and evaluate their own hypotheses.

Paul M. Kellstedt is Professor of Political Science at Texas A&M University. He is the author of *The Mass Media and the Dynamics of American Racial Attitudes* (Cambridge, 2003), winner of Harvard University's John F. Kennedy School of Government's 2004 Goldsmith Book Prize. In addition, he has published numerous articles in a variety of leading journals. He is the Editor-in-chief of *Political Science Research and Methods*, the flagship journal of the European Political Science Association.

Guy D. Whitten is Cullen-McFadden Professor of Political Science, as well as Director of the European Union Center, at Texas A&M University. He has published a variety of articles in leading peer-reviewed journals. He is on the editorial boards of *Political Analysis* and *Political Science Research and Methods*.

An R Companion for the Third Edition of The Fundamentals of Political Science Research

Paul M. Kellstedt
Texas A&M University

Guy D. Whitten
Texas A&M University

CAMBRIDGE
UNIVERSITY PRESS

CAMBRIDGE
UNIVERSITY PRESS

University Printing House, Cambridge CB2 8BS, United Kingdom

One Liberty Plaza, 20th Floor, New York, NY 10006, USA

477 Williamstown Road, Port Melbourne, VIC 3207, Australia

314–321, 3rd Floor, Plot 3, Splendor Forum, Jasola District Centre,
New Delhi – 110025, India

79 Anson Road, #06–04/06, Singapore 079906

Cambridge University Press is part of the University of Cambridge.

It furthers the University's mission by disseminating knowledge in the pursuit of
education, learning, and research at the highest international levels of excellence.

www.cambridge.org
Information on this title: www.cambridge.org/9781108446037
DOI: 10.1017/9781108601832

© Paul M. Kellstedt and Guy D. Whitten 2021

First published 2021

A catalogue record for this publication is available from the British Library.

ISBN 978-1-108-44603-7 Paperback

Additional resources for this publication at www.cambridge.org/FPSR-R

BRIEF CONTENTS

CONTENTS

Preface

We received a wealth of useful feedback from instructors and students about the first two editions of *The Fundamentals of Political Science Research*. In response to feedback on the first edition, we substantially increased the number of end-of-chapter exercises in the second edition. While the response to this increase was positive, we sensed a demand for even more exercises and, in particular, more hands-on material for how to put the techniques that we discuss in the book into action. This workbook is our attempt to meet these demands. It is one of three workbooks, each written to help students to work with the materials covered in *The Fundamentals of Political Science Research, Third Edition* using a particular piece of statistical software.

This workbook focuses on using the program R from another program, RStudio. Our expectation is that the modal user of this book will be using a relatively recent version of R and RStudio.

The chapter structure of this workbook mirrors the chapter structure of the third edition of *The Fundamentals of Political Science Research*. We have written with the expectation that students will read the chapters of this companion after they have read the chapters of the book.

We owe a special thank you to Andrea Junqueira for her help with the writing of R code for this workbook.

We continue to update both the general and instructor-only sections of the webpage for our book (www.cambridge.org/fpsr). As before, the general section contains data sets available in formats compatible with SPSS, Stata, and R. The instructor-only section contains several additional resources, including PowerPoint and TEX/Beamer slides for each chapter, a test-bank, and answer keys for the exercises.

FIGURES

1 THE SCIENTIFIC STUDY OF POLITICS

1.1 OVERVIEW

In this chapter we introduce you to some of the important building blocks of a scientific approach to studying politics. As you can already tell from reading the first chapter of the Third Edition of *The Fundamentals of Political Science Research* – which we will refer to as *"FPSR"* from here on – data are an important part of what we do both to explore the political world and to test hypotheses based on causal theories. An important part of working with data is learning how to use a statistical software package. In the sections that follow, we introduce you to the R program and some basics that you will need to get up and running. In doing this, we also introduce some general principles of good computing practices for effectively working with data.

1.2 "A WORKBOOK? WHY IS THERE A WORKBOOK?"

You might be asking yourself this question, and it's perfectly fair to do so. Allow us to try to explain how this workbook fits in with the main *FPSR* text.

As you will see in the weeks and months to follow in your class, the main textbook will teach you about the use of statistics in political science, mostly by using equations and examples. So yes, in some ways, it will feel rather math-y. (And we think that's cool, though we realize that it's not everyone's cup of tea.) One of the ways that people learn about the practice of statistics is to use computer software to calculate statistics directly. To that end, many instructors want students to learn to use a particular computer software package so they can begin to conduct statistical analyses themselves.[1] We have discovered through years of teaching that this transition between equations in a book and software output on a computer screen is a very difficult one. The goal of this software companion book is to make this connection stronger, even seamless.

If we are successful, this book will do two things. First, it will teach the nuts and bolts about how to use R. Though many (perhaps most) students today are quite computer-literate, we believe that having a reference guide for students to learn the techniques, or for them to teach themselves out of class time, will be helpful. Second, and more importantly, this software guide will provide explicit hand-holding to you as you learn

---

[1] This particular software companion book teaches students to use R, but we have also produced parallel books for instructors who wish to have their students learn SPSS or Stata.

to connect the key principles from the main text to the practical issues of producing and interpreting statistical results.

Each chapter of this software guide works in parallel with that of the main *FPSR* text. So when you learn the equations of two-variable regression analysis in Chapter 9 of the main text, you will learn the details about using R to estimate two-variable regression models in Chapter 9 of this companion book. And so on. In the end, we hope that the very important (but perhaps rather abstract) equations in the text become more meaningful to you as you learn to estimate the statistics yourself, and then learn to interpret them meaningfully and clearly. Those three things – formulae, software, and interpretation – together provide a very solid foundation and basic understanding of social science.

1.2.1   Reading Commands in This Workbook

Throughout this workbook, when we present R commands in their text versions, we will write out commands in typewriter type to help distinguish actual R commands from our instructional text. For instance,

```
summary(Reg1)
```

is an example of a command that we would issue if we had previously estimated a regression model which we called "Reg1" and we wanted R to produce a summary table of the results. Occasionally, we will also use italics within a command line to indicate a place in the code where something needs to be placed, but where the exact text of the command depends on what the user is trying to accomplish with that command. So, for instance, in the next chapter where we demonstrate one way to install a new package using the "install.packages" command, we will write the following code:

```
install.packages("PackageName")
```

where "*PackageName*" is not what one should enter into the command line (there is not a package named "*PackageName*"), but rather a placeholder written in italics to indicate that one should enter in that part of the code the name of the package that they want to install.

1.3   GETTING STARTED WITH R AND RSTUDIO

To get started with R and RStudio, we recommend that you set yourself up in front of a computer that has both of the programs installed with a copy of the third edition of *FPSR* close by. You should also have the set of computer files that accompany this text (which you can download from the text's website, www.cambridge.org/fpsr) in a directory on the computer on which you are working. You will get the most out of this workbook by working in RStudio as you read this workbook.

The instructions in this book can help you learn R whether you use a Windows-based PC or a Mac. Once the program is launched, R in RStudio works identically, no matter which platform you use. Mac users should be aware, though, that our screenshots will come from a Windows-based PC. Some of those screenshots that involve finding and opening files on your computer, therefore, will look somewhat unfamiliar to Mac users, but we assume that Mac users are at least somewhat used to this. Overall, the differences between running R in RStudio on Windows compared to a Mac are minimal.

Finally, we wrote this book while using versions 4.0.3 of R and the free version of RStudio 1.3.1093. Particularly for the statistical fundamentals you will learn in this book, the differences between versions are not severe. But, since both programs are available for free and easy to install, we recommend that you use the versions that we are using or a newer version of these programs.

1.3.1   Launching RStudio

When you are sitting in front of a computer on which RStudio and R have been properly installed, you can launch the program by double-clicking on the RStudio icon or by finding the RStudio program on your start menu. At this point, you should see one large window like that in Figure 1.1. Within this main window, you will see three other windows labeled "Console" (on the left side), "Environment" (on the top right side), and "Plots" (on the bottom right side). If you are seeing all of this, you are ready to go.

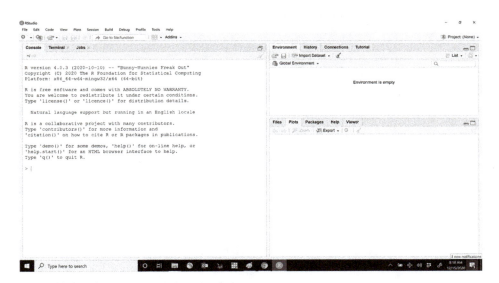

Figure 1.1 RStudio initial launch

1.3.2   Getting R to Do Things

In almost any mainstream statistical program today, there are multiple ways to accomplish the same tasks. In R in RStudio, the two most common ways to execute commands are by typing them in the console next to the blue > symbol or by typing them into a script in the editor, selecting the command, and hitting the "run" button. The choice of which of these options to use is a matter of personal comfort. But, as we discuss below, no matter which way you choose to get R to do things, you need to keep track of what you are doing. We now discuss the two ways to get R to do things by showing an example of opening a data set. We recommend that you try both, but especially the example of using a script in this section.

Typing Commands in the Console Window

You can type commands directly into the console window that you see on the left side of RStudio when you launch the program. These commands are typed in one at a time and are executed by the program when you hit the "Enter" button on your keyboard.

So, if you want to load the data set "EcoVote" which is an R-format data set (with the ".RData" suffix), you would type the following command into the "Console" window and hit the "Enter" key on your computer:

```
load("C:/MyFPSRrFiles/EcoVote.RData")
```

To check whether you have done this correctly, you can click the tab labeled "Environment" in the upper-right window of RStudio. If you have successfully loaded the data, your RStudio will look like Figure 1.2 where we now see the name of the data set that we were attempting to load and a brief summary of how many observations and variables are in the data set.[2]

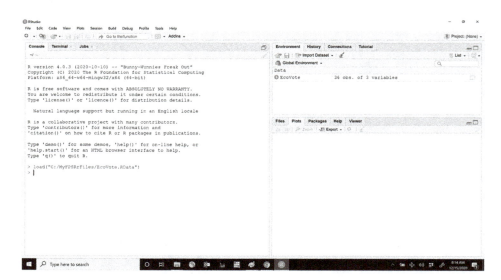

Figure 1.2 Data set successfully loaded into R

---

[2] The location of files is often a stumbling block for beginner users of a statistical software package. To keep things simple, we recommend that you create a folder on your computer's C drive named "MyFPSRrFiles" and put all of the files that you have downloaded from www.cambridge.org/fpsr into that folder. If you are unable to do this, then on a computer using a Windows operating system you can find the exact name of the location of a file by right-clicking on that file, left-clicking "Properties," and then looking at the entry to the right of "Location." This filepath, or location, can be selected, copied, and pasted directly into your console window (or script) to insure that it is exactly right. But, it is important to note that the slashes to tell R the location of a file are forward slashes instead of the usual Windows convention of using backslashes.

Using a Script File

A second way to issue commands in RStudio is to use a script file. While this method of working will seem a little bit clumsy at first, it is our preferred method of working in RStudio for reasons that we will explain below. To start work with a new script file, you need to left-click on the "file" tab in the very upper-left corner of the program, and then from the menu that drops down select "New File," followed by "R Script." Once you have successfully done this, your RStudio should look like Figure 1.3. We will eventually cover a lot of different things that one can do with a script file, but for now, all that we want you to do is to type the following command into the new script file:

```
load("C:/MyFPSRrFiles/EcoVote.RData")
```

Once you have typed this command into the script-file editor, you can then select the entire line – you can do this by left-clicking at the beginning of the line and then moving to the end and releasing the left mouse button – and then click on the "Run" button at the right side of the top of the script-file editor window that has a green arrow pointing from a box toward the word "Run." Clicking on this button tells the program to execute the selected line or lines of code.[3] In Figure 1.4, we show what this will look like right before you click on "Run." Once you have done this correctly, your RStudio should look like Figure 1.5. And, to further check that you did this correctly, when you left-click on the "Environment" tab in the upper-right corner window, you should see the same contents in that window as what you see in Figure 1.5.

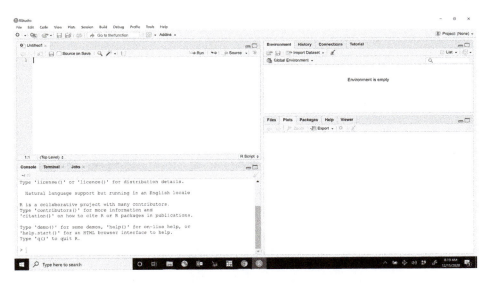

Figure 1.3 Script editor window open

---

[3] This also works for selecting multiple lines of code, as we do later in this file. It is worth noting two additional things. First, you don't have to select the entire line of code to submit it as long as your cursor is located somewhere in the line that you wish to run. And second, instead of clicking the "Run" button, you can run code by hitting the Control and Enter keys at the same time (Ctrl + Enter).

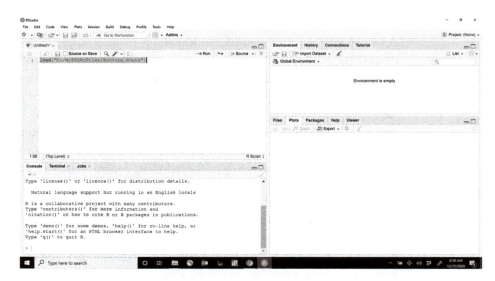

Figure 1.4 Preparing to execute a command from the script-file editor

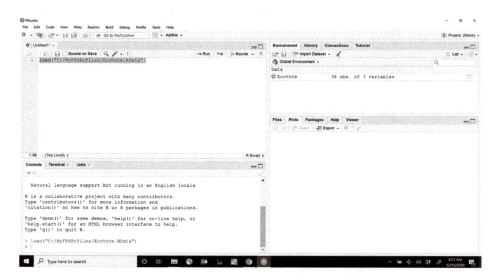

Figure 1.5 RStudio after having successfully run a command from the script-file editor

1.3.3   Initially Examining Data in R

Now that we have shown you two different ways to get a data set into R, we want you
to take a look at the data that you have loaded into the program. These data are from
a famous study of economic voting conducted by Ray Fair (Fair 1978). They contain
values of economic growth and incumbent party vote from US presidential elections
between 1876 and 2016. To get an initial look at these data, click on "EcoVote" in the
Environment window in the upper-right corner of RStudio. Once you have done this,
your RStudio should look like Figure 1.6. Each column in this spreadsheet contains

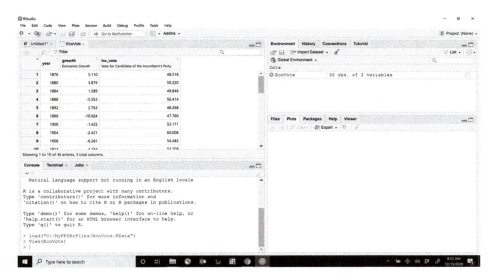

Figure 1.6 Initially examining data in RStudio

values for a single variable and each row contains data from a single election. You are now ready to proceed to the end-of-chapter exercises.

1.3.4   Adding Notes to Script Files and Saving Them

The main advantage of script files is that they can be saved. This allows users to go back later and see exactly what they did. Once you start writing longer script files, it is a good idea to make notes in them about what you are doing and why you are doing it. We can make notes in script files by starting the line on which we want to write notes with a hash symbol (#). When you ask RStudio to run a command line that starts with #, R reads that symbol as "ignore everything to the right of this symbol on this line of code" and, appropriately, does nothing. This is known as "commenting out a line" of code. This is helpful when we want to submit an entire script file to R at one time but still have notes about what we did. The programs that are available on the webpage for our book (`www.cambridge.org/fpsr`) contain commented-out lines that explain what is going on in them.[4]

In Figure 1.7 we have clicked back on the R script that we created to load our data set and saved it as a file named "LoadData.R." Notice that we have added a comment at the top of the script file, preceded by a # that tells us what this script is. It is normally a good idea to add additional lines of comments that identify the person who wrote the code and the date on which the script file was created.

---

[4] You may also want to use the # symbol to add a note to part of a line of code. In this case, you would just put whatever note you want to add to the right of the # and anything that you don't wish to comment out to the left of the #.

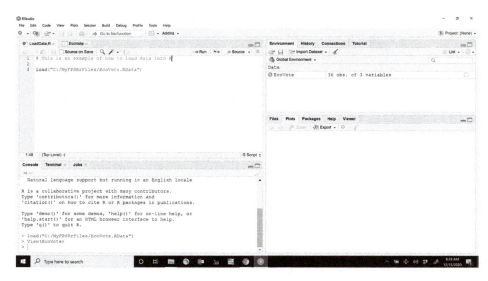

Figure 1.7 Script with comment line saved

1.4   EXERCISES

1.   Go through all of the steps described above. Once you have the data set open (so that your computer looks like Figure 1.6), do the following:

(a)   Look at the values in the column labeled "growth." This is Fair's measure of percentage change in real GDP per capita. Do the following:

i.   Identify the year with the highest value for this variable.

ii.   Identify the year with the lowest value for this variable.

iii.   What does it mean if this variable goes up by 1?

(b)   Look at the values in the column labeled "inc_vote." This is Fair's measure of the percentage of major party votes cast for the party of the president at the time of the election. Now do the following:

i.   Identify the year with the highest value for this variable.

ii.   Identify the year with the lowest value for this variable.

iii.   What does it mean if this variable goes up by 1?

2 THE ART OF THEORY BUILDING

2.1 OVERVIEW

One of our emphases in the book has been on producing new causal theories, and then evaluating whether or not those theories are supported by evidence. In this chapter, we describe how to explore sources of variation – both across space, and across time – to get you started thinking about new explanations for interesting phenomena. We also help you explore how new theories can be built upon the existing work in the literature. Before we can explore data, however, we need to do a little bit of work in R to get access to the commands that we will use.

2.2 R PACKAGES

One of the great things about R is that the user community is constantly producing new tools for everyone using the program. These new tools are made available in the form of programming modules called "packages." Once you have R and RStudio installed on your computer, you can add additional packages in at least the following three different ways:

1. By left-clicking on the "Tools" located in the upper-left corner of RStudio, and then selecting "Install Packages." This will launch a pop-up window in which you should type the name of the package that you wish to install and then left-click the "Install" button.

2. By left-clicking on the word "Packages" at the top of the bottom-right window. You then see a list of packages that you already have installed on your computer. From there, you can select the search window (next to a magnifying glass) to allow you to search for a particular package and install it.

3. By running the following command (either from the console or from a script file):
   `install.packages("PackageName")`

At the time that we are preparing this guide, there are over 10,000 packages available for R. In order to do all of the things that we discuss in this book, you will need the following packages:

- tidyverse
- gmodels
- labelled
- psych
- lm.beta
- car

In Figure 2.1 we can see a script written to install all of these packages. Note that, depending on the speed of your computer and your connection to the Internet, this script might take some time to run. You can tell that it has finished when you see a blue > symbol at the bottom of the console window like what we see in Figure 2.1.

It is worth noting that every time you start an RStudio session, you will need to tell the program which packages you wish to use. This is done with a "library" command. For instance,

```
library(tidyverse)
```

tells R to load the package "tidyverse," which is a package that provides access to a large set of commands that all follow a similar structure.[1]

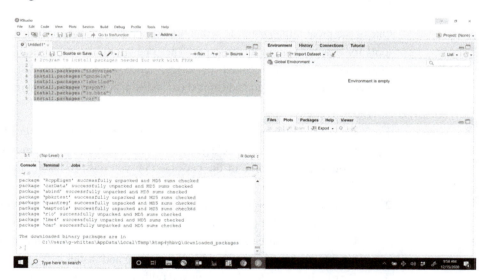

Figure 2.1 Packages installed by script

2.3   EXAMINING VARIATION ACROSS TIME AND ACROSS SPACE

As we discuss in Section 2.3 of *FPSR*, one way to develop ideas about causal theories is to identify interesting variation. In that section, we discuss examining two types of

---

[1] Tidyverse is actually a collection of packages. For more information on this, visit www.tidyverse.org

variation, cross-sectional and time-series variation. In this section, we show you how to create figures like the ones presented in Section 2.3 of *FPSR*. Although there are many different types of graphs that can be used to examine variation in variables, we recommend a bar graph for cross-sectional variation and a connected plot for time-series variation.

As you will see from these examples, R's graph commands can often be quite long because of all of the options that we typically like to include. We therefore recommend that you start with the main command and then add the options until you get a figure that looks right to you. For the example of the bar graph, we go through steps along these lines in some detail. In later presentations, we will show the final product.

2.3.1   Producing a Bar Graph for Examining Cross-Section Variation

A useful way to get a sense of the variation for a cross-sectional variable is to produce a bar graph in which you display the values of that variable across spatial units. In the example that we display in Figure 2.1 of *FPSR*, we have a bar graph of military spending as a percentage of gross domestic product in 2005 for 22 randomly selected nations. Building on what we have learned about R so far, we will now show you how to produce a figure like this. First, we need to load the tidyverse package:

```
library(tidyverse)
```

The second step is to load in the data:

```
load("C:/MyFPSRrFiles/milspend_pct_05.RData")
```

which will load the appropriate data set into R. Once you have this data set properly loaded into R, you will want to issue a command to produce a bar graph of the variable milspend_pct for each spatial unit. In this case, the spatial unit is nation. A command for producing such a bar graph is:

```
ggplot(data=milspend_pct_05, aes(x=nation, y=milspend_pct)) +
geom_bar(stat="identity") +
theme_bw()
```

where "ggplot" tells R that we want to use the ggplot package. The next part of the command, "milspend_pct," is the name of the data set that we wish to use. The "aes" is short for "aesthetic mappings," which is a way of communicating to the program which variables are going to play what roles in the figure that we wish to create. In this case, since we are producing a bar graph, we use "y" to tell R the name of the variable for which we wish to display the values in bars, milspend_pct, and "x" to tell R the name of the variable for which the bars will reflect spatial units or cases, nation. The "+" is entered into the script as a part of the ggplot syntax which tells R that we are going to add some new features to the plot.[2] Continuing on the second line, geom_bar tells R that we want to produce a bar graph, stat="identity" tells R that

---

[2] Unlike the default settings for other statistical programs, in R you do not need to add special characters to tell the program that a command extends over multiple lines.

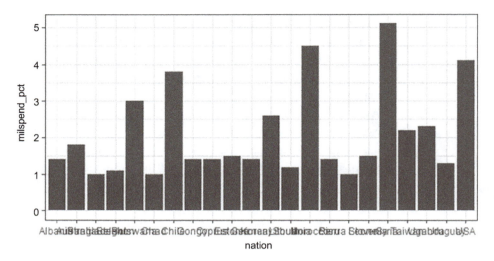

Figure 2.2 Initial bar graph of military spending

we want to use the value of y to determine the height of the bars, and `theme_bw()` tells R that we want to use a simple graph theme with black bars on a white background with grid lines in the background. The resulting graph from this command is displayed in Figure 2.2.

One problem that we can see right away in Figure 2.2 is that it is all but impossible to read the names of the countries along the bottom of the horizontal axis. We can fix this by adding to our code as follows:

```
ggplot(data=milspend_pct_05, aes(x=nation, y=milspend_pct)) +
geom_bar(stat="identity") +
theme_bw() +
theme(axis.text.x = element_text(angle=30, hjust=1, vjust=1))
```

where the additional line of code tells R that we want to adjust the `theme` further by changing the horizontal axis text, `axis.text.x`, such that each element is now at a 30 degree angle, (`angle=30, hjust=1, vjust=1`). The resulting graph is displayed in Figure 2.3.

Compare Figure 2.3 with Figure 2.1 in *FPSR*. What is the difference between these two figures? The answer is that in Figure 2.1 in *FPSR* the values of military spending have been sorted from smallest to largest. When displaying data in graphs, it is important that you do so in a fashion that allows you and your readers to most easily make the assessments that they want to make. In this case, since we are trying to think about what makes a country spend more or less of its GDP on its military, we want to be able to see which countries spend more or less. Try comparing the value of military spending between Belgium and Lithuania in the graph that we just made, Figure 2.3. Not an easy thing to do! It's a lot easier using Figure 2.1 from *FPSR* because the cases have been *sorted*. You might have also noticed that the label on the vertical axis in Figure 2.1 from *FPSR* is more communicative. We can make these two adjustments by writing the command as

```
ggplot(data=milspend_pct_05,
aes(x=reorder(nation, milspend_pct), y=milspend_pct)) +
geom_bar(stat="identity") +
theme_bw() +
theme(axis.text. x = element_text(angle=30, hjust=1, vjust=1)) +
ylab("Military Expenditures as a Percentage of GDP") +
xlab("")
```

where x=reorder(nation, milspend_pct) tells R to sort the bars based on the value of the variable milspend_pct, ylab("Military Expenditures as a Percentage of GDP") produces a more informative label on the vertical axis, and xlab("") removes the unnecessary horizontal axis label. The figure that this code produces is not identical to Figure 2.1 in *FPSR* because that figure was created in Stata, but it is very similar.

All of the commands for this example are contained in a script file called "Chapter 2 Bar Graph Example.R" which can be found in the MyFPSRrFiles directory.

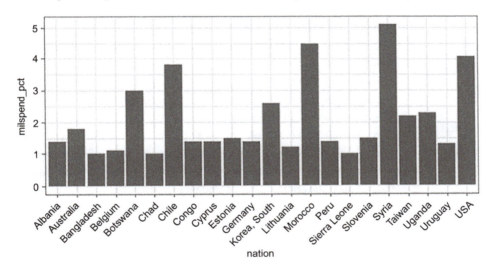

Figure 2.3   Initial bar graph of military spending with angled nation names

2.3.2   Producing a Connected Plot for Examining Time-Series Variation

A useful way to get a sense of the variation for a time-series variable is to produce a connected plot in which you display the values of that variable *connected* across time. In the example that we display in Figure 2.2 of *FPSR*, we have a connected plot of the values for US presidential approval each month from February 1995 to December 2005. Building on what we learned so far, we will now show you how to produce a figure like this in R. As with the previous example, the first step to doing this is to run commands to load the required packages and the data:

```
library(tidyverse)
load("C:/MyFPSRrFiles/presap9505.RData")
```

The command for producing Figure 2.2 of *FPSR* is

```
presap9505 %>%
mutate(date_seq = seq(1:nrow(presap9505))) %>%
ggplot(aes(x=date_seq, y=presap)) +
geom_line() +
geom_point() +
theme_bw() +
scale_x_continuous(breaks = seq(6,119, by=6),
labels = presap9505$year_month[seq(6,119, by=6)]) +
ylab("Presidential Approval") +
xlab("Year/Month")
```

This is a fairly complex command which involves first taking the data set that we have loaded, mutating it, and then producing a plot of the resulting data. The "%>%" at the end of the first line of this command tells R that the data object to use is named "presap9505." On the second line of code, it is mutated such that a new variable date_seq is created which is a numeric sequence counting from the top of the first row of data to the bottom. The "%>%" at the end of the second line of this command tells R that the resulting data object is now going to be put through another process. In this case, that process is a plot created by ggplot. We see an aes statement, again, short for "aesthetic mappings," which tells R that the horizontal axis with the newly created date_seq variable and the vertical axis will be presap, which is the presidential approval variable. The next two lines tell R to create two different graphs, geom_line() which is a line graph and geom_point() which is a dot plot. The combination of these two graph types shows the exact points of data connected by a line, which is a good way to depict both the individual values of the variable and their progression over time, two essential elements for observing variation across time. The next two lines tell R how to label the horizontal axis, with labels every six months using the original date variable "year_month" as the horizontal axis labels. And the last two lines tell R how to label the y and x axes.

In Chapter 12, we will introduce you to a series of commands associated with time-series data and some other ways in which to produce graphs of time-series data. All of the commands for this example are contained in a script file called "Chapter 2 Connected Graph Example.R" which can be found in the MyFPSRrFiles directory.

2.4   USING GOOGLE SCHOLAR TO SEARCH THE LITERATURE EFFECTIVELY

We assume that you're skilled at web searches, likely using Google's search engine. In addition to the myriad other things that Google allows us to search for on the Internet, it has a dedicated search engine for scholarly publications like books and journal articles. The aspects of Google you're likely most familiar with come from Google's home page – www.google.com. The searches that they enable through scholarly work, however, using what they call "Google Scholar," are at a different site: scholar.google.com. That site looks a good bit like Google's home page, but when you're at Google Scholar, it's searching a different corner of the Internet entirely – the part where academic journals and books are uploaded.

Figure 2.4 shows the Google Scholar home page. If you have a Google account (like a gmail address), you can save items in "My Library" – we'll show you how to do that shortly – that you can access any time. The articles are normally saved as Adobe .PDF files. You'll notice the familiar search box that looks like Google's normal home page. You can tell from the figure, though, that despite the similarities in appearances, this website is `scholar.google.com`.

So let's see how Google Scholar works. In the first chapter of *FPSR*, we introduced you to what we called the theory of economic voting. The seminal article in the study of economic voting was conducted by an economist named Ray Fair. So let's see what happens when we type "Ray Fair economic voting" in the Google Scholar search bar.

Figure 2.4 The Google Scholar home page

Figure 2.5 shows the results of that Google Scholar search. As luck would have it, the first search result happens to be that path-breaking article. Let's examine that result. If you look to the far right of the selection, you see the text "[PDF] jstor.org," which shows you what format the file is available in – in this case, an Adobe .PDF – and where – in this case, at the archive `jstor.org`. Your college or university's library almost surely has a subscription to JStor that your student fees pay for, and so if you're on a campus internet connection (as opposed to a WiFi network at your home, or on a cellular network), clicking on "[PDF] jstor.org" will take you to the article. (If you're on your home WiFi network, then JStor doesn't know that you're a university student, and the publisher might ask you to pay a rather steep fee for access to the article. So beware about where you can do these searches for free.)

There's a lot of other information that the Google Scholar search reveals, though. First, if you want to save the Ray Fair article to your "My Library," then click on the ★ at the lower left of the item, and you'll be able to access that .PDF anywhere.

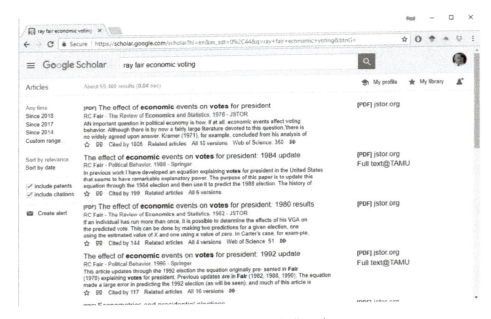

Figure 2.5 Google Scholar results for "Ray Fair economic voting" search

Importantly, you can also see how influential every article has been to date. In Figure 2.5, you can see text near the bottom of the citation that says "Cited by 1005" – which means that the Fair article has been cited 1005 times to date.[3] That number indicates that the paper has been massively influential.[4]

Of course, that doesn't necessarily mean that 1005 other articles all cite the Fair article approvingly. Some might; others might not. But being agreed with, or being "proved right," isn't the highest value in science. It's far better to be an influential part of an ongoing debate while being proved wrong in some respects, then it is to be indisputably correct but ignored by other scholars.

Perhaps you say to yourself, "Sure, Professor Fair wrote an influential article on economic voting a good long while before I was born. What kind of work is being done on the topic *now*?" This is one of the places where Google Scholar is fabulous. That "Cited by 1005" is clickable. You can literally see the list of all 1005 articles that cite the Fair article if you want. (Of course, it would take you a while to sift through them!)

Figure 2.6 shows the results when you click the "Cited by 1005," and then click the "Since 2017" option on the left side of the screen. (You can pick "since" any year you like, obviously.) Just beneath the search bar in Figure 2.6, you'll see the text in light gray

---

[3] If you go conduct that same search today, the number would surely be higher; our search was conducted on January 9, 2018. Citations tend to accumulate over time.

[4] Of course, you should be careful to remember the original publication date when interpreting citation counts as a measure of impact. Fair's article was published in 1978, so it's not as if some scholars who work in this area have somehow not yet heard of his article. But for an article published more recently – say in 2016 – its impact cannot yet fully be known. That merely means that we don't yet know if the article is likely to have a large impact. Only time will tell.

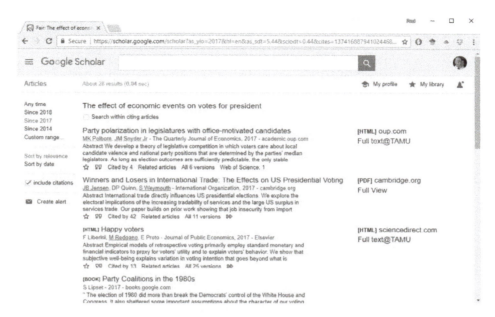

Figure 2.6 Google Scholar search results of articles citing Ray Fair (1978) article

saying "About 28 results," indicating that, since 2017, the Fair article has been cited by 28 other articles. So it continues to have influence today.

This is a good way to start the process of exploring a particular topic in academic writing that interests you. This example began by having us tell you that the initial article that spawned all of this interest was written by Ray Fair. So we incorporated his name, obviously, into the search terms. Often, to be sure, this isn't the case.

Just like with using any internet search engine, there's something of a skill in figuring out how to efficiently search for the material you want without getting bogged down with lots of results that aren't interesting to you. Should you use quotation marks in your search, or in a portion of your search terms? Sometimes yes, sometimes no. (In the example above, we did not.) As a general rule, it might be best to try it both ways to see if you get different results.

We have not exhausted all there is to know about how to use Google Scholar here, of course. For example, many scholars have created "Google Scholar profiles," which enables you to see the list of scholarly articles and books that they have authored, usually sorted from those with the most citations to the ones with the least. This can help you find similar articles, too, because many scholars work on a topic over the course of many years, and therefore their earlier articles are related to their more recent ones. In Figure 2.6, for example, you can see the scholars whose names are underlined; those are clickable links to those scholars' respective Google Scholar profiles. In addition, the "Help" section of Google Scholar is surprisingly helpful![5]

---

[5] In light gray text, you can see the "Help" link that you can click in the bottom-right of Figure 2.4.

2.5   WRAPPING UP

In the main text, we discussed how important it is that our theories be new and original – that is, that we aren't merely repeating the ideas and claims of previous scholars. One of the important preconditions for doing something genuinely new is to be familiar with the works that have already been produced on that same topic. Having the vast archive of journal articles and even many books available online – and freely accessible, thanks to your university's libraries – through storage sites like `www.jstor.org` has been the first step in making this task a lot easier than it was in decades past. The second step has been the invention of very sophisticated search engines like Google Scholar to help us find the previous studies that we otherwise might have missed.

2.6   EXERCISES

1. Conduct a search for the following terms using both Google's homepage (`www.google.com`) and Google Scholar (`scholar.google.com`). Only include the quotation marks in your search if we include them. Report the similarities and differences you observe in the first page of the search results:
    (a) "presidential approval"
    (b) "nuclear proliferation"
    (c) nuclear proliferation
2. Open the script file named "Chapter 2 Bar Graph Example.R" in RStudio. Make sure that you have the correct directory path for loading the data. In other words, if "C:\MyFPSRrFiles" is not where you have your data, change this part of the script file so that the data load into RStudio.
    (a) Once you have done this, run the code to produce the graph presented in Figure 2.1 from *FPSR*. Open a word processing document and then copy the figure from R and paste it into your word processing document.
    (b) Write a short summary of what you see in this figure.
3. Open the script file named "Chapter 2 Connected Graph Example.R" in RStudio. Make sure that you have the correct directory path for loading the data. In other words, if "C:\MyFPSRrFiles" is not where you have your data, change this part of the script so that the data load into RStudio.
    (a) Once you have done this, run the code to produce the graph presented in Figure 2.2 from *FPSR*. Open a word processing document and then copy the figure from R and paste it into your word processing document.
    (b) Write a short summary of what you see in this figure.

3 EVALUATING CAUSAL RELATIONSHIPS

3.1 OVERVIEW

Unlike the previous two chapters, in Chapters 3 through 5, there will not be any computer-based lessons in R or elsewhere. Not to worry, though. There will be more than enough time for intensive computer work later in the book. We promise!

In this abbreviated chapter, then, we offer some expanded exercises that will apply the lessons learned in the main text, and build on the skills from the first two chapters.

3.2 EXERCISES

1. Causal claims are common in media stories about news and politics. Sometimes they are explicitly stated, but often they are implicit. For each of the following news stories, identify the key causal claim in the story, and whether, based on the information given, you are convinced that all four causal hurdles have been crossed. (But remember that most media stories aren't the original generators of causal claims; they merely report on the news as they see fit to do so.)

   (a) www.cnn.com/2018/01/16/politics/freedom-house-democracy-trump-report/index.html

   (b) thehill.com/opinion/energy-environment/368355-wheres-the-proof-climate-change-causes-the-polar-vortex

   (c) www.foxnews.com/us/2018/01/16/california-mudslides-where-and-why-happen.html

   (d) www.aljazeera.com/news/2018/01/trump-muslim-ban-shifted-public-opinion-study-finds-180113092728118.html

   (e) www.npr.org/player/embed/575959966/576606076 (Podcast)

2. Candidates for public office make causal claims all the time. For each of the following snippets from a key speech made by a candidate, identify the key causal claim made in the speech, and whether, based on the information given, you are convinced that all four causal hurdles have been crossed. (But remember that candidates for office are not scientists responsible for testing causal claims; they are trying to persuade voters to support them over their opponent.)

   (a) America is one of the highest-taxed nations in the world. Reducing taxes will cause new companies and new jobs to come roaring back into our country. Then we are going to deal with the issue of regulation, one of the greatest job-killers of them all. Excessive regulation is costing our country as much as $2 trillion a year, and we will end it. We are going to lift the restrictions on the production of American energy. This will produce more than $20 trillion in job creating economic activity over the next four decades. (Excerpt from Donald Trump's speech accepting the Republican nomination for President, July 21, 2016.)

(b)   Now, I don't think President Obama and Vice President Biden get the credit they deserve for saving us from the worst economic crisis of our lifetimes. Our economy is so much stronger than when they took office. Nearly 15 million new private-sector jobs. Twenty million more Americans with health insurance. And an auto industry that just had its best year ever. That's real progress. (Excerpt from Hillary Clinton's speech accepting the Democratic nomination for President, July 28, 2016.)

(c)   The truth is, on issue after issue that would make a difference in your lives – on health care and education and the economy – Sen. McCain has been anything but independent. He said that our economy has made "great progress" under this president. He said that the fundamentals of the economy are strong. And when one of his chief advisers – the man who wrote his economic plan – was talking about the anxiety Americans are feeling, he said that we were just suffering from a "mental recession," and that we've become, and I quote, "a nation of whiners." (Excerpt from Barack Obama's speech accepting the Democratic nomination for President, August 28, 2008.)

(d)   His [Barack Obama's] policies have not helped create jobs, they have depressed them. And this I can tell you about where President Obama would take America: His plan to raise taxes on small business won't add jobs, it will eliminate them; ... And his trillion-dollar deficits will slow our economy, restrain employment, and cause wages to stall. (Excerpt from Mitt Romney's speech accepting the Republican nomination for President, August 30, 2012.)

3.   Political science, as we have argued, revolves around the making and evaluation of causal claims. Find each of the following research articles – Google Scholar makes it easy to do so – and then identify the key causal claim made in the article. Then produce a causal hurdles scorecard, and decide to what degreee you are convinced that all four causal hurdles have been crossed. Some of the statistical material presented in the articles will, this early in the semester, be beyond your comprehension. That will change as the semester rolls along! (And remember that political scientists are trained to be experts in testing causal claims. So set the bar high.)

(a)   Heberlig, E., Hetherington, M., and Larson, B. 2006. "The price of leadership: Campaign money and the polarization of congressional parties." *Journal of Politics* 68(4):992–1005.

(b)   Stasavage, D. 2005. "Democracy and education spending in Africa." *American Journal of Political Science* 49(2):343–358.

(c) De Mesquita, B.B., Morrow, J.D., Siverson, R.M., and Smith, A. 1999. "An institutional explanation of the democratic peace." *American Political Science Review* 93(4):791–807.

(d) Lipsmeyer, C.S. and Pierce, H.N. 2011. "The eyes that bind: Junior ministers as oversight mechanisms in coalition governments." *Journal of Politics* 73(4):1152–1164.

4 RESEARCH DESIGN

4.1 OVERVIEW

As was the case in Chapter 3, there will not be any computer-based lessons in R or elsewhere. Again, we offer some expanded exercises that will apply the lessons learned in the main text.

4.2 EXERCISES

1. There are a lot of substantive problems in political science that we might *wish* to study experimentally, but which might seem to be impossible to study with experimental methods. (Recall from the main text (Section 4.2.4) that one of the drawbacks to conducting experiments is that not all X variables are subject to experimental control and random assignment.) Imagine the following causal questions, and write a paragraph about what would be required to conduct an experiment in that particular research situation, being careful to refer to both halves of the two-part definition of an experiment in your answer. (Warning: Some of them will seem impossible, or nearly impossible, or might require time travel.)

   (a) Does the development of state-sponsored universities cause economic development to rise?

   (b) Has the establishment of independent central banks to control monetary policy caused a reduction in the severity of recessions?

   (c) Does an individual's religiosity cause a person's level of opposition to same-sex marriage?

   (d) Does a country's openness to trade cause blue-collar workers' wages to fall?

   (e) Does having a more professionalized legislature cause states to respond more quickly to voters' preferences?

   (f) Does having a more racially diverse set of school administrators and teachers cause a reduction in student suspensions and expulsions?

2. For each of the above research situations, if you were *unable* to perform an experiment, name at least one potential Z variable that could potentially confound the $X - Y$ relationship, and would need to be controlled for in some other manner, in an observational study.

3.   Assuming that you were unable to conduct an experiment for the aforementioned research situations, describe an observational study that you might conduct instead. In each case, is the study you envision a cross-sectional or time-series observational study? Why?

4.   Consider the following research question: Does exposure to stories in the news media shape an individual's policy opinions?

   (a)   Write a short paragraph trying to explain the causal mechanism that might be at work here.

   (b)   If we wanted to study this relationship using an experiment, what would the barriers to conducting the experiment be?

   (c)   What, if any, are the ethical considerations involved in studying that relationship experimentally?

   (d)   What are the benefits of exploring that relationship experimentally? In other words, what specific Z variables would be controlled for in an experiment that could potentially be confounding in an observational study?

   (e)   Go read the following article and write a one-paragraph summary of it:

   - King, Gary, Benjamin Schneer, and Ariel White. 2017. "How the news media activate public expression and influence national agendas." *Science* 358:776–780.

5.   Consider the relationship between the level of democracy in a country and the country's respect for human rights.

   (a)   Describe both a cross-sectional and a time-series observational design that would help test the theory that increases in the level of democracy cause a country to increase its respect for human rights.

   (b)   What concerns would you have about crossing the four causal hurdles in each case?

6.   Using the model described in Section 4.4 of the main text, write a one-paragraph summary of the following research articles:

   (a)   Stasavage, David. 2005. "Democracy and education spending in Africa." *American Journal of Political Science* 49(2):343–358.

   (b)   O'Brien, Diana Z. 2015. "Rising to the top: Gender, political performance, and party leadership in parliamentary democracies." *American Journal of Political Science* 59(4):1022–1039.

   (c)   Fortunato, David, Randolph T. Stevenson, and Greg Vonnahme. 2016. "Context and political knowledge: Explaining cross-national variation in partisan left-right knowledge." *Journal of Politics* 78(4):1211–1228.

   (d)   Titiunik, Rocio. 2016. "Drawing your senator from a jar: Term length and legislative behavior." *Political Science Research and Methods* 4(2): 293–316.

   (e)   Bansak, Kirk, Jens Hainmueller, and Dominik Hangartner. 2016. "How economic, humanitarian, and religious concerns shape European attitudes toward asylum seekers." *Science* 354(6309): 217–222.

5   MEASURING CONCEPTS OF INTEREST

5.1   OVERVIEW

As was the case in Chapters 3 and 4, there will not be any computer-based lessons in R or elsewhere. Again, we offer some expanded exercises that will apply the lessons learned in the main text.

5.2   EXERCISES

1. Consider, for a moment, the concept of "customer satisfaction." For now, let's define it as "the degree to which a product or service meets or exceeds a customer's expectations." So, like other concepts, it is a variable: Some customers are very satisfied, some have mixed experiences, and some are very unhappy. Companies – and even some government agencies – are interested for obvious reasons in understanding that variation. Now answer the following questions:

   - How well do you think Yelp reviews serve as a measure of customer satisfaction? Explain your answer.
   - Go read "The Happiness Button" in the Februray 5, 2018 issue of *The New Yorker*: www.newyorker.com/magazine/2018/02/05/customer-satisfaction-at-the-push-of-a-button. What are the strengths and weaknesses of the strategy pursued by HappyOrNot in terms of measuring the concept of customer satisfaction?
   - The article describes the push button measures of satisfaction at security checkpoints in London's Heathrow Airport. What are the strengths and weaknesses of such an approach? If, on a particular day, there was a higher share of "frown" responses, what would that tell (and what wouldn't that tell) to the officials at Heathrow?

2. The concept of "political knowledge" is a very important one in the study of public opinion and political behavior, as it lies at the heart of many influential theories of why citizens hold the opinions that they do, and why they vote the way that they do. Answer the following questions:

   - Conceptually, how would you define political knowledge? Try to be as specific as possible.

- Measuring political knowledge, as you might imagine, can be a bit tricky. For years, the American National Election Studies (ANES) measured the concept by asking a small list of factual questions about politics. The questions were of the form:

  Now we have a set of questions concerning various public figures. We want to see how much information about them gets out to the public from television, newspapers and the like... [NAME] — What job or political office does he [or she] NOW hold?

  Survey respondents were not given a closed-ended list of response options from which to choose; instead, they were allowed to respond freely, and their responses were recorded verbatim. After the survey was completed, coders would look at the response transcript and judge whether the answers were correct or not. A respondent's score on the political knowledge scale, then, would be the sum total of the number of correct answers given. What are the various strengths and weaknesses of such an approach?
- Go skim the following report from the ANES, which pertains to these types of survey questions: `www.jstor.org/stable/pdf/24572671 .pdf`. What were the main problems identified with the survey items? What effects did it have in measuring political knowledge?
- In more recent surveys, the ANES has been asking different types of survey questions to measure political knowledge. These questions are closed-ended, and for most, respondents are given a fixed list of options from which to choose. Here are two examples from the 2012 survey:

  On which of the following does the US federal government currently spend the least? [Response Options (in random order): Foreign aid; Medicare; National defense; Social security.]

  For how many years is a United States Senator elected—that is, how many years are there in one full term of office for a US Senator? [No response options given; exact number recorded.]

  What are the potential strengths and weaknesses of this revised strategy to measure political knowledge?
- Can you think of an alternative measurement strategy for this concept?

3. The concept of "consumer confidence" is important in the study of Economics and Political Science, among other disciplines.

    - Go to `news.google.com` and search for "consumer confidence" (and be sure to use the quotation marks). From the search results, pick a recent news article that discusses consumer confidence. (Print out the article and include it with your homework.) How well, if at all, does the article define consumer confidence, or how it is measured?
    - From what you know, offer a conceptual definition of consumer confidence.
    - There are two major surveys in the US that measure consumer confidence on monthly intervals. One of them is the Survey of Consumers at the University

of Michigan. They produce what they call an Index of Consumer Sentiment, which is composed of responses to five survey items. One of the five is as follows:

Looking ahead, which would you say is more likely—that in the country as a whole we'll have continuous good times during the next five years or so, or that we will have periods of widespread unemployment or depression, or what?

What are the potential strengths and weaknesses of this survey question as one component of consumer confidence?

- All five of the items in the Michigan Index of Consumer Sentiment can be found here: `data.sca.isr.umich.edu/fetchdoc.php?docid=24770`. How are the five items similar to one another, and how are they different from one another?

- The complete monthly survey can be found here: `data.sca.isr.umich .edu/fetchdoc.php?docid=24776`. You will note that the survey does not contain *any* questions to measure a survey respondent's political beliefs or affilitations. Why do you think that is the case?

- Can you think of any additional survey questions that might complement or replace the ones in the Michigan Index?

6 GETTING TO KNOW YOUR DATA

6.1 OVERVIEW

In this chapter we introduce you to the commands needed to produce descriptive statistics and graphs using R in RStudio. If you're feeling a little rusty on the basics of R and RStudio that we covered in Chapters 1 and 2, it would be good to review them before diving into this chapter.

In Chapter 6 of *FPSR* we discussed a variety of tools that can be used to get to know your data one variable at a time. In this chapter, we discuss how to produce output in R to allow you to get to know your variables. An important first step to getting to know your data is to figure out what is the measurement metric for each variable. For categorical and ordinal variables, we suggest producing frequency tables. For continuous variables, there are a wide range of descriptive statistics and graphs.

6.2 DESCRIBING CATEGORICAL AND ORDINAL VARIABLES

As we discussed in Chapter 6 of *FPSR*, a frequency table is often the best way to numerically examine and present the distribution of values for a categorical or ordinal variable. In R, the "CrossTable" command is used to produce frequency tables. In a script file or from the console command line, the syntax for this command is

```
CrossTable(datasetname$variablename)
```

where *datasetname* is the name of the data set and *variablename* is the name of the variable for which you want the frequencies. When issued like this, this command produces a table with two rows and one column for each unique value for the variable. In the first row, the variable values are displayed and, in the second row, we see the number and the proportion of cases that take on that value in the chosen data set. The data presented in Table 6.1 of *FPSR* are an example of the output obtained from using the "CrossTable" command. These results were generated using the data set ANES2004small.Rdata which can be found in the R directory at www.cambridge.org/fpsr. The output from this use of the CrossTable command is displayed in Figure 6.1. Take a moment to compare the table in Figure 6.1 with Table 6.1 of *FPSR*. Although both tables convey the same information, Table 6.1 of *FPSR* does so in a more polished fashion. This is an example of why we don't want to copy from the RStudio output and paste that into our papers or presentations. Instead, it is important to craft tables so that they convey what is most necessary and don't include a lot of extra information. We'll have more to say about making tables in Chapter 8 (and forward) in this workbook.

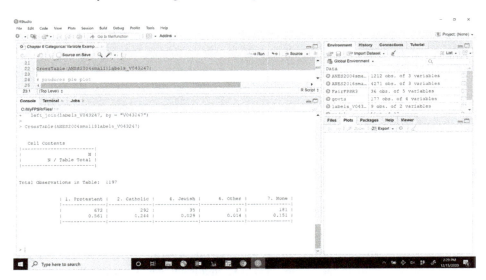

Figure 6.1 Raw output from CrossTable command

Pie graphs, such as Figure 6.1 in *FPSR*, are a graphical way to get to know categorical and ordinal variables. The command to produce a pie graph in a script file or from the console command line using the same data as Figure 6.1 is

```
ggplot(subset(ANES2004small, !is.na(ANES2004small$labels_V043247)),
aes(x="", y=V043093,
fill=gsub(".*\\.","",labels_V043247))) +
geom_bar(stat="identity", width=1) +
coord_polar("y", start=0) +
theme_void() +
scale_fill_gray() +
theme(legend.title = element_blank())
```

where the first line of code tells R to use only those cases for which the religious self-identification variable (V043093) is not missing, the second line tells R how to adjust the value labels for this variable,[1] the third line tells R that we are going to produce a type of bar graph, the fourth line tells R that the specific form of bar graph will be displayed on a polar coordinate system (thus a pie graph), the fifth and sixth lines tell R about the theme and colors, and the seventh line tells R how to create the legend. The output in RStudio from this command is displayed in Figure 6.2. It is nearly identical to Figure 6.1 in *FPSR* which was produced in Stata.

---

[1] The labels in the data were "1.Catholic", "2.Jewish", etc. The "gsub" function is for replacing text characters in a data set. So, "gsub" combined with ".*\\." tells R to delete everything before "." and the period. That way, we end up with "Catholic", instead of "1.Catholic".

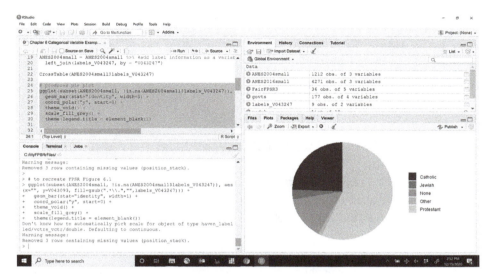

Figure 6.2 R pie graph

As we discuss in Chapter 6 of *FPSR*, statisticians strongly prefer bar graphs to pie charts because bar graphs, especially when they have been sorted by the frequency with which the value occurs, make it easier for one to make assessments about the relative frequency of different values. As an example of how to obtain a figure like this in R, we can run the following code:

```
ANES2004small %>%
group_by(V043247) %>%
mutate(count_religion = n()) %>%
dplyr::select(V043247, count_religion) %>%
distinct() %>%
drop_na() %>%
ggplot(aes(x=reorder(V043247, -count_religion), y = count_religion)) +
geom_bar(stat="identity") +
theme_bw()
```

where the first six lines of code rearrange the data objects and the last three produce the bar chart displayed in Figure 6.3. Note, though, that Figure 6.3 is not exactly like Figure 6.2 of *FPSR*. To produce this figure, we need the following command:

```
ANES2004small %>%
group_by(V043247) %>%
mutate(count_religion = n()) %>%
dplyr::select(V043247, count_religion, labels_V043247) %>%
distinct() %>%
drop_na() %>%
ggplot(aes(x=reorder(gsub(".*\\.","",labels_V043247), -count_religion),
y = count_religion)) +
geom_bar(stat="identity") +
```

```
theme_bw() +
xlab("") +
ylab("Number of Cases")
```

which adds value labels and a vertical axis label.

6.3   DESCRIBING CONTINUOUS VARIABLES

While the values for categorical variables in a sample of data can easily be presented in a frequency table, this is usually not the case for continuous variables. Consider Table 6.2 in *FPSR*. Even for a relatively small data set, such as that presented in Table 6.2 in *FPSR*, this output provides a lot of information and it is difficult to see any patterns. For this reason, we turn to summary statistics when we want to describe continuous variables. To use a metaphor, with summary statistics, we are looking at the broad contours of the forest rather than examining each individual tree.

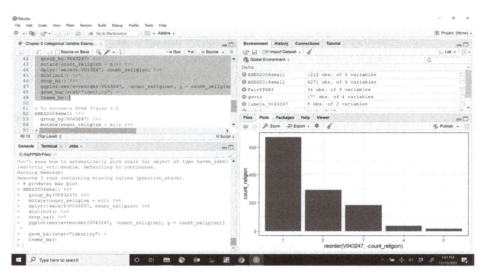

Figure 6.3 R bar chart

Figure 6.3 in *FPSR* displays the output from Stata's "summarize" command with the "detail" option. As we discuss in the book, this command produces a full battery of descriptive statistics for a continuous variable. To produce similar output in R, we can use the following command:

```
FairFPSR3 %>%
select(inc_vote) %>%
drop_na() %>%
summarise(Mean = mean(inc_vote), SD = sd(inc_vote), N = n(),
Min = min(inc_vote), Max = max(inc_vote), Quantiles = quantile(inc_vote,
c(0, 0.25, 0.5, 0.75, 1)))
```

where the first three lines of code tell R to remove all cases with missing values while making the calculations in the next two lines of code. The results from this code are displayed in Figure 6.4. Note that the mean, standard deviation (SD), minimum (min), and maximum (max) are all repeated in each row and the rank values are displayed in the final column.

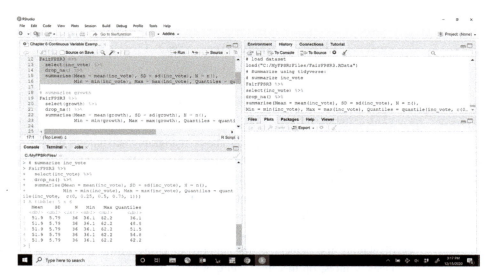

Figure 6.4 R summary statistics

While statistical summaries of variables are helpful, it is also quite helpful to also look at visual summaries of the values for a continuous variable. To get a visual depiction of rank statistics, we recommend producing a box-whisker plot like that displayed in Figure 6.4 in *FPSR*. The syntax for a box-whisker plot of the values for a single continuous variable (in this case incumbent vote) is

```
ggplot(FairFPSR3, aes(y=inc_vote)) +
geom_boxplot(fill="gray", color="black") +
theme_bw() +
theme(axis.title.x=element_blank(),
axis.text.x=element_blank(),
axis.ticks.x=element_blank()) +
ylab("Incumbent Vote Percentage")
```

To get a visual depiction of moment statistics, we recommend producing either a histogram – as in Figure 6.5 and 6.6 from *FPSR* – or a density plot – Figure 6.7 from *FPSR*. The syntax in R for producing a histogram like Figure 6.5 from *FPSR* is

```
ggplot(FairFPSR3, aes(x=inc_vote)) +
geom_histogram(breaks=c(35,40,45,50,55,60,65), aes(y=..density..),
colour="black", fill="gray") +
scale_x_continuous(breaks=c(35,40,45,50,55,60,65)) +
theme_bw() +
xlab("Incumbent Vote Percentage") +
ylab("Density")
```

The syntax in R for producing a density plot like Figure 6.6 from *FPSR* is

```
ggplot(FairFPSR3, aes(x=inc_vote)) +
geom_density() +
theme_bw() +
xlab("Incumbent Vote Percentage") +
ylab("Density")
```

When students are learning about histograms and kernel density plots, a frequent question that they have is, "Which is better?" We don't have a definitive answer to this question. Both histograms and kernel densities are graphical ways for summarizing the distribution of values for one variable in a sample data set. As such, they both simplify reality. The histogram does this by dividing the different values for the variable being depicted into ranges called "bins" that look like the bars in a bar graph and then displaying the density of the number of cases within each of these ranges or bins. Density plots, on the other hand, produce a more smoothed depiction of the contours of the forest of values for the variable being summarized. To go back to the metaphor that we started with, both histograms and kernel density plots are trying to summarize the broad shape of the forest and thus miss some of the details of individual trees. If you're having difficulty choosing which one you like better, one option is to put them both in the same figure. We can do this in R with the following code:

```
ggplot(FairFPSR3, aes(x=inc_vote)) +
geom_histogram(breaks=c(35,40,45,50,55,60,65), aes(y=..density..),
colour="black", fill="gray") +
scale_x_continuous(breaks=c(35,40,45,50,55,60,65)) +
theme_bw() +
xlab("Incumbent Vote Percentage") +
ylab("Density") +
geom_density()
```

6.4 PUTTING STATISTICAL OUTPUT INTO TABLES, DOCUMENTS, AND PRESENTATIONS

So you've generated some statistical output for the first time. Congratulations! But now what do you do? As you can tell from the descriptions above, we think it's important to be thoughtful about how to present your results to your audience. That's why we went to great lengths to show you commands to make the graphics appear in the most interpretable way possible. The same is true with data that you wish to include in a tabular format. We emphasize that just copying and pasting output from RStudio (or any other program) is unlikely to impress your audience – even if your audience is "just" your professor or TA.

For example, when we produce descriptive statistics in R, we get a *lot* of output. Usually this output is much more than what we need to present in a paper that describes our variables one at a time. We therefore suggest making your own tables in whatever word processing program you are working with.

Graphs are a bit simpler, though. Once you have a graph that meets the standards we've outlined above, and you want to include in a document, one of the easiest ways to do this is to select the "plot" tab in the lower-left window of RStudio and then click on the button labeled "Export." At this point, you can save your graph as a separate file or choose "copy to clipboard" and then right-click on the location where you want to place the graph in your word processing program and select "paste." Depending on the word processor, you might want to resize the graphic image by clicking on the corner of the image and dragging the image to be bigger or smaller, depending on what would look best in your paper or presentation.

We'll have more to say about this topic in Chapter 8, and forward, as we introduce new statistical techniques to you. The upshot, though, is always the same: put some care into what you present to your audience. The amount of attention you devote to the details – low or high – will be obvious to them.

6.5 EXERCISES

1. Open the script file named "Chapter 6 Categorical Variable Example.R" in RStudio. Make sure that you have the correct directory path for loading the data. In other words, if "C:\MyFPSRrFiles" is not where you have your data, change this part of the script file so that the data load into Rstudio.

   Once you have done this, run the code to produce the graphs presented in Figures 6.1 and 6.2 from *FPSR*. Open a word processing document and then copy these figures from RStudio and paste them into your word processing document.

2. Run a CrossTable command for variable V043093 which is each respondent's prediction of who will win the 2004 US presidential election. In your word processing document, create a frequency table like Table 6.1 from *FPSR* for variable V043093.

3. Create a pie chart and a bar graph like Figures 6.1 and 6.2 from *FPSR* for variable V043093. Copy these figures from RStudio and paste them into your word processing document.

4. Write a short summary of what you see in the table and figures that you created using variable V043093.

5. Open the script file named "Chapter 6 Continuous Variable Example.R" in RStudio. Make sure that you have the correct directory path for loading the data. In other words, if "C:\MyFPSRrFiles" is not where you have your data, change this part of the script file so that the data load into RStudio.

Once you have done this, run the code to create a box-whisker plot, a histogram, kernal density plot, and a combined histogram and kernel density plot. Copy and paste each of these figures into your word processing document.

6. Produce summary statistics for the variable "growth," which is the percentage change in real (meaning that this measure is adjusted for inflation) Gross Domestic Product (GDP) per capita (meaning that it has been adjusted for population). Make a table in your word processing document which contains the moment statistics for this variable.

7. Produce a box-whisker plot for the variable "growth."

8. Produce a histogram, kernal density plot, and a combined histogram and kernel density plot for the variable "growth." Copy and paste each of these figures into your word processing document.

9. Write a short summary of what you see in the table and figures that you created using variable "growth."

7 PROBABILITY AND STATISTICAL INFERENCE

7.1 OVERVIEW

The goal of this chapter is to familiarize you with some of the basics of how probability works, and especially to see how sample sizes come into play. To do this, we take advantage of R's facilities for random number generation.

7.2 DICE ROLLING IN R

To simulate rolling a six-sided die and see the results, we can run the following command:

```
sample(1:6, 1, replace=TRUE)
```

which tells R that we want to make a single random draw from whole numbers from 1 to 6. The "sample" function tells R that we wish to randomly generate data, the "1:6" tells R the values from which we want random draws, and then, after a comma, we tell R that we want to sample one value. The statement "replace=TRUE" tells R that we want to do sampling with replacement. Technically, this doesn't matter in this particular instance because we are asking for only a single draw. But, if we were doing multiple draws, this statement would matter. If instead of "replace=TRUE" we wrote "replace=FALSE," we would be sampling without replacement and each number could only be chosen one time. In Figure 7.1 we can see the result from running this command. The result from the depicted single trial, which is displayed in the console window, was a value of "2." Every time you run this command, R will make a new independent draw from whole numbers from 1 to 6.

To see some of the example ideas about probability in action, we can build more complicated simulations. We will start with a simulation of a single six-sided die being rolled 60 times. What should we expect to see from such a simulation? Because we know that each whole number has an equal probability of being selected on each roll/draw and there are six whole numbers from 1 to 6, we should expect to see each number come up ten times. To run this simulation and look at the results, we issue the following two commands:

```
roll60 <- sample(1:6, 60, replace=TRUE)
ggplot() +
geom_bar(aes(as.factor(roll60)),
fill = "white", color = "black") +
xlab("roll60")
```

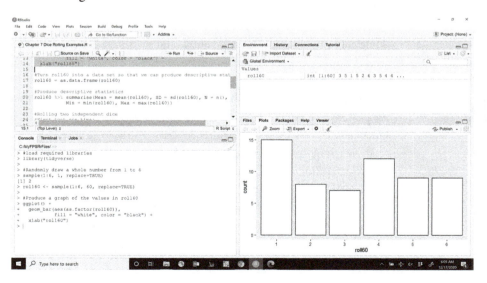

Figure 7.1 Simulating a single roll of a six-sided die

The first command creates a data element, "roll60," which we can see in the "Environment" tab in the upper-right corner of RStudio. That element is generated by the "sample" command after which the only change from our first simulation command is that we change the number of draws from 1 to 60.

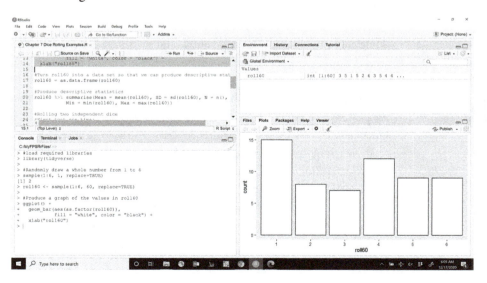

Figure 7.2 Simulating 60 rolls of a six-sided die

The results from running these two lines of code are displayed in Figure 7.2. As you can see, we have now changed the number of dice rolls from 1 to 60 and created a new data element named "`roll60`" that appears under the "Environment" tab in the upper-right window. As with the previous command, every time we run the first command, the results will change. In this case, the data element `roll60` will be replaced, meaning that the distribution of the rolls across the six possible outcomes will vary. The second command, which begins with "`ggplot`," should be mostly familiar. What it does is create a bar graph of the data element `roll60` which appears in the lower-right corner of RStudio as depicted in Figure 7.2. The *x* axis in the figure represents the six sides of the die, and the *y* axis represents the number of the rolls that came out with that number. Of course, when you run these commands on your own computer, you will get a different outcome, because the presented results are the result of random forces. In our simulated rolls, however, what you'll notice is that we rolled fewer 3s than we would have expected – 7 when we would have expected 10 of the rolls to come up 3. Among other things, the figure also reveals that, randomly, we rolled more 1s – 15 – than would have been predicted by chance. Such is the nature of randomness.

Looking over Figure 7.2, you might have noticed that the entry for the data element roll60 in the "Environment" tab doesn't look like what we saw in that tab for data sets that we loaded into R in earlier chapters. In order to turn it into a data set on which we can calculate descriptive statistics, we need to run the following command:

```
roll60 = as.data.frame(roll60)
```

Now, using what we learned in Chapter 6, we can get R to produce descriptive statistics using the following command:

```
roll60 %>% summarise(Mean = mean(roll60), SD = sd(roll60), N = n(),
Min = min(roll60), Max = max(roll60))
```

What should we expect for the mean of these 60 rolls?[1] From the lower-right console window in Figure 7.3, we can see that it is 3.32, a little lower than we expected. The

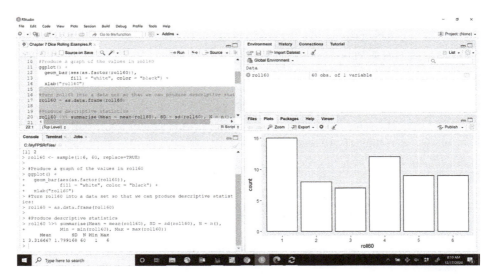

Figure 7.3 Descriptive statistics from 60 rolls of a six-sided die

---

[1] The correct answer is 3.5.

standard deviation – which, as you will recall, measures how tightly clustered or how widely dispersed the scores are – is 1.8.

Using the results of the Central Limit Theorem from the textbook, we can use these numbers to create a confidence interval for the likely value of the population mean based on what we have observed in our sample. To do that, we need to calculate the standard error of the mean. You may recall that the formula for the standard error of the mean ($\sigma_{\bar{Y}}$) is:

$$\sigma_{\bar{Y}} = \frac{s_Y}{\sqrt{n}},$$

where s_Y is the sample standard deviation and n is the sample size. In our case, that equals:

$$\sigma_{\bar{Y}} = \frac{1.8}{\sqrt{60}} = 0.23.$$

To create an approximate 95% confidence interval for the likely value of the population mean, you will recall that we can use the rule of thumb that we would go 2 standard errors in both directions to obtain the interval. In other words:

$$\bar{Y} \pm 2 \times \sigma_{\bar{Y}} = 3.32 \pm (2 \times 0.23) = 3.32 \pm 0.46.$$

That means, based on what we've observed in our sample, we are 95% confident that the population mean for our rolls of the die lies somewhere on the interval between 2.86 and 3.78. And, there is a 2.5% chance that the true population mean is below 2.86, and a 2.5% chance that the true population mean is above 3.78.

Of course, you'll be able to tweak this exercise by varying the number of rolls of the die. When you do, it will change that number in the denominator. And, the larger the sample size, the larger the denominator in the formula for the standard error, which means that the resulting quotient will be smaller. That smaller quotient translates to a tighter (smaller) confidence interval. This is how larger sample sizes reduce our uncertainty about the true value of the population characteristics in which we're interested.

Let's do one more example. Say that instead of rolling one die, we rolled two dice at the same time. What would we expect the sum of the two dice to be?[2] To simulate the rolling of two dice at once, we can use the following command:

```
replicate(2, sample(1:6, 1, replace=T))
```

This tells R that we want to "replicate" the original "sample" command two times. In Figure 7.4, we can see that we rolled two sixes, for a total of 12.

---

[2] The correct answer is 7.

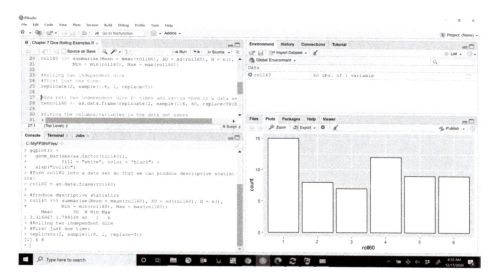

Figure 7.4 Simulating rolling two six-sided dice at once

How likely is this outcome?[3] Let's repeat this random draw 60 times to get an approximate answer. We can do this through the following commands (we have left comment notes, preceded by a # symbol, above each command to explain what it does):

```
#Now roll two independent dice 60 times and saving them in a data set
tworoll60 <- as.data.frame(replicate(2, sample(1:6, 60, replace=TRUE)))

#Giving the columns/variables in the data set names
colnames(tworoll60) <- c("die 1", "die 2")

#Creating a new variable that is the sum of each pair of die rolls
tworoll60$sum <- tworoll60$'die 1'+tworoll60$'die 2'

#Plotting the 60 sums
tworoll60 %>% ggplot() +
geom_bar(aes(as.factor(sum)),
fill = "white", color = "black") +
xlab("sum")

#Obtaining descriptive statistics on the sums
tworoll60 %>% summarise(Mean = mean(sum), SD = sd(sum), N = n(),
Min = min(sum), Max = max(sum))
```

In Figure 7.5, we can see the results from running all of these commands from a script file. In the plot in the lower-right corner, the *x* axis represents the sum of the rolls of the two die, which has a hypothetical range between 2 and 12. Though, because we did

---

[3] It's actually highly unlikely and should occur in only one out of 36 rolls of two six-sided dice or 2.8% of the time.

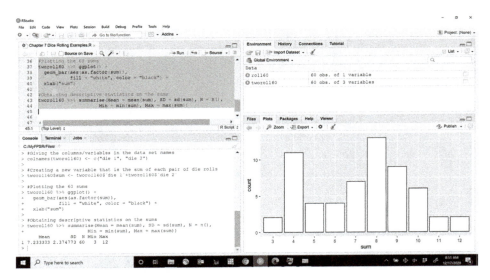

Figure 7.5 Simulating rolling two six-sided dice at once 60 times

not observe any double-ones, the range in this plot is from 3 to 12. As before, the *y* axis displays the number of rolls in each category. The pattern, we're sure you'll notice, is quite different in Figure 7.5 than it was in Figure 7.2, in which we rolled only one die.

7.3   EXERCISES

1.   Open the script file named "Chapter 7 Dice Rollings Examples.R" in RStudio. Write commands to simulate the rolling of a single six-sided die 500 times. Produce a histogram of the output, and calculate the mean and standard deviation of the sample. On the basis of those results, calculate (by hand) the 95% confidence interval for the population mean.

2.   Make a table with three columns named "die one," "die two," and "sum." In each row, enter one of the possible outcomes of rolling two dice and the sum from that outcome (note, a 3, 2 is a different outcome than 2, 3). Using this table, do the following:

   (a)   Add up all of the entries in the "sum" column and divide by the number of unique outcomes from rolling two dice (the number of rows in your table). Write this number and explain what it is.

   (b)   What is the probability of rolling double-sixes?

3.   Use the commands discussed in this chapter which are located in "Chapter 7 Dice Rollings Examples.R" to show the effects of the sample size on the size of the confidence interval for the population mean by simulating rolling the two six-sided dice the following number of times:

   (a)   9 times

   (b)   25 times

   (c)   100 times

(d)   400 times

(e)   1,600 times

(f)   2,500 times

Describe in some detail the nature of the effects of sample size on the amount of uncertainty we have connecting a sample to the underlying population. **Bonus:** Use RStudio to input data into two variables. Let the first variable be the sample sizes above, and the second variable be the resulting standard error of the mean. Plot the relationship graphically. (Hint: You might need to peek ahead to Chapter 8 to see how to do this!)

4.   For the above question, how (if at all) does changing the sample size affect the calculated sample means and standard deviations? Can you explain why?

8   BIVARIATE HYPOTHESIS TESTING

8.1   OVERVIEW

We are now ready to start testing hypotheses! As we discuss in Chapter 8 of *FPSR*, bivariate hypothesis tests, or hypothesis tests carried out with only two variables, are seldom used as the primary means of hypothesis testing in political science research today. But it is imperative to understand the basic mechanics of bivariate hypothesis tests before moving to more complicated tests. This same logic applies to the use of statistical computing software. In this chapter, we teach you how to conduct hypothesis tests using the three techniques presented in Chapter 8 of *FPSR*: tabular analysis, difference of means, and the correlation coefficient.

8.2   TABULAR ANALYSIS

In tabular analysis, we are testing the null hypothesis that the column variable and row variable are unrelated to each other. We will review the basics of producing a table in which the rows and columns are defined by the values of two different variables, generating hypothesis-testing statistics, and then presenting what you have found.

The R syntax for producing a two-variable table is

```
CrossTable(rowvariable, columnvariable)
```

where "*rowvariable*" is usually the dependent variable (with its values displayed across rows in the table) and "*columnvariable*" is usually the independent variable (with its values displayed down the columns in the table). The values displayed from top to bottom in each cell are as follows: the number of cases, the chi-squared contribution of that cell, the row percentage, the column percentage, and the percentage of total cases. As detailed in Chapter 8 of *FPSR*, the column percentages allow for the comparison of interest – they tell us how the dependent variable values differ in terms of their distribution across values of the independent variable. It is crucial, when working with tables of this nature, to put the appropriate variables across the rows and columns of the table and then to present the column frequencies. For example, to recreate Table 8.2 in *FPSR* we first run the command

```
CrossTable(ANES2016small$V2Trump, ANES2016small$unionHH)
```

where "V2Trump" is a categorical variable that takes on a value of "1" if the respondent reported voting for Donald Trump and "0" if the respondent reported voting for Hillary Clinton, and "unionHH" is a variable that takes on a value of "1" if the respondent reported that someone in their household belonged to a union and "0" otherwise. The output from this running command is displayed in Figure 8.1. Take a moment to compare this raw output with Table 8.2 in *FPSR*. There are three notable differences. First, in order to isolate the numbers needed for the assessment at hand (whether or not voters from union households voted differently from voters from non-union households in the 2016 election), we need only the column percentages. Second, instead of the names of the variables from the output ("V2Trump" and "unionHH") and the numbers reflecting their values ("1" and "0"), we have provided more intuitive labels for the variables and their values. And, third, we have added a note making it clear what are the values reported in each cell of the table.

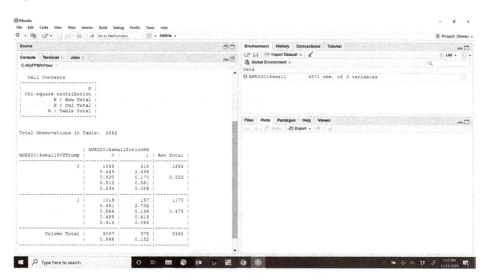

Figure 8.1 Raw output from CrossTable command

8.2.1   Generating Test Statistics

In Chapter 8 of *FPSR* we discuss in detail the logic of Pearson's chi-squared test statistic which we use to test the null hypothesis that the row and column variables are not related. To get this test statistic and the associated p-value for a two-variable table in R we can use the following command

```
CrossTable(rowvariable, columnvariable, chisq = T)
```

where, again, "*rowvariable*" is usually the dependent variable (with its values displayed across rows in the table) and "*colvariable*" is usually the independent variable (with its values displayed down the columns in the table). The ", chisq=T" (which is shorthand for chi-squared=True) tells R to report a chi-squared test statistic and the associated p-value. Thus to conduct the chi-squared test reported in Section 8.4.1 of *FPSR*, we would issue the command

```
CrossTable(ANES2016small$V2Trump, ANES2016small$female, chisq = T)
```

which produces the output displayed in Figure 8.2.

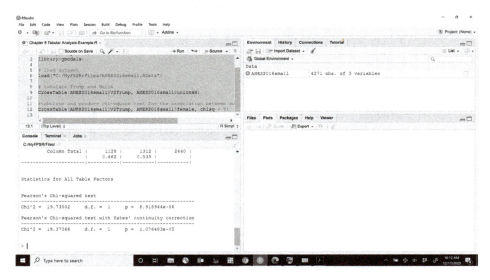

Figure 8.2 Raw output from CrossTable command with a chi-squared test

8.2.2   Putting Tabular Results into Papers

We recommend that you make your own tables in whatever word processing program you choose to use instead of copying and pasting the tables that you make in RStudio. The first reason for doing so is that you will think about your results more closely when you are producing your own tables. This will help you to catch any mistakes that you might have made and to write more effectively about what you have found. Another reason for doing so is that tables constructed by you will tend to look better. By controlling how the tables are constructed, you will be able to communicate with maximum clarity.

As a part of making your own tables, you should have the goal in mind that your table communicates something on its own. In other words, if someone *only* looked at your table, would they be able to figure out what was going on? If the answer is "yes," then you have constructed an effective table. We offer the following advice ideas for making useful tables:

- Give your table a title that conveys the essential result in your table
- Make your column and row headings as clear as possible
- Put notes at the bottom of your table to explain the table's contents

8.3 DIFFERENCE OF MEANS

Difference of means tests are conducted when we have a continuous dependent variable and a limited independent variable.

8.3.1 Examining Differences Graphically

When we use graphs to assess a difference of means, we are graphing the distribution of the continuous dependent variable for two or more values of the limited independent variable. Figure 8.1 of *FPSR* shows how this is done with a box-whisker plot. The code for producing a plot like Figure 8.1 of *FPSR* is[1]

```
ggplot(govts, aes(x=as.factor(mingov) ,y=govttime)) +
geom_boxplot(fill="gray", color="black") +
scale_x_discrete(labels = c("Majority", "Minority")) +
theme_bw() +
xlab("") +
ylab("Number of Days in Government")
```

where the variable "govttime" is the number of days each government lasted in office and "mingov" is a catgeorical variable equal to 1 if the government was a minority government and equal to 0 otherwise.

In Figure 8.2 of *FPSR* we produced a density plot of the distribution of our continuous dependent variable for the two values of our limited independent variable. The code for producing Figure 8.2 of *FPSR* is the following:[2]

```
ggplot(govts, aes(x=govttime, color=as.factor(mingov))) +
geom_density() +
theme_bw() +
scale_color_manual(name = "Government", labels = c("Majority",
"Minority"), values = c("gray", "black")) +
xlab("Number of Days in Government")
```

8.3.2 Generating Test Statistics

To conduct a difference of means t-test such as the one discussed in Chapter 8 of *FPSR*, the syntax is:

```
t.test(govttime ~as.factor(mingov), data = govts, var.equal = T)
```

---

[1] The figure in *FPSR* was created using Stata, so there will be some slight differences between that and what you produce using R in RStudio.
[2] The figure in *FPSR* was created using Stata, so there will be some slight differences between that and what you produce using R in RStudio.

which produces the output displayed in the console window in the bottom-left corner of Figure 8.3. From this we can see that we have reproduced exactly the main result from the difference of means t-test presented in Chapter 8 of *FPSR*.

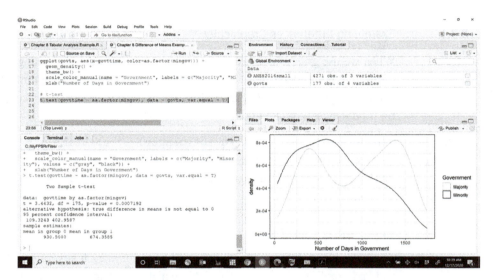

Figure 8.3 Raw output from a difference of means test

8.4   CORRELATION COEFFICIENTS

Correlation coefficients summarize the relationship between two continuous variables. They are also an important building block to understanding the basic mechanics of two-variable regression models.

8.4.1   Producing Scatter Plots

We can examine the relationship between two continuous variables in a scatter plot such as Figure 8.3 in *FPSR*. We can reproduce the main features in Figure 8.3 in *FPSR* with the following command:

```
ggplot(FairFPSR3, aes(x=growth, y=inc_vote)) +
geom_point() +
theme_bw()
```

where "geom_point()" tells R that we want to produce a scatter plot. The results from this command are displayed in the plot window in the lower-right part of Figure 8.4.

The command for producing Figure 8.3 in *FPSR* is[3]

```
ggplot(FairFPSR3, aes(x=growth, y=inc_vote)) +
geom_point(shape=1) +
theme_bw() +
xlab("Percentage Change in Real DGP Per Capita") +
ylab("Incumbent Party Vote Percentage")
```

where "geom_point(shape=1)" tells R to make hollow circles instead of the default filled in circles that we see in Figure 8.4. These symbols make it a little bit easier to see overlapping data points.

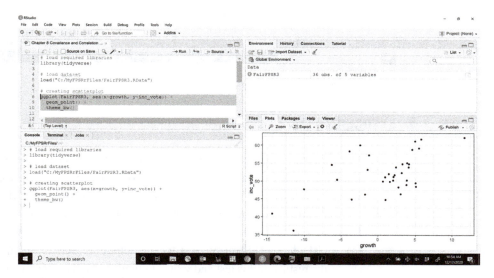

Figure 8.4 Basic output from scatter command

8.4.2   Generating Covariance Tables and Test Statistics

To generate the output for a covariance table like Table 8.13 in *FPSR*, the command is

```
cov(FairFPSR3[, c("inc_vote", "growth")], use = "complete.obs")
```

To generate a correlation coefficient using these same variables, the command is

```
cor(FairFPSR3[, c("inc_vote", "growth")], use = "complete.obs")
```

And, to calculate the t-test presented in *FPSR*, the command is

```
cor.test(FairFPSR3$inc_vote, FairFPSR3$growth, use = "complete.obs")
```

which generates the output that we see in Figure 8.5.

---

[3] The figure in *FPSR* was created using Stata, so there will be some slight differences between that and what you produce using R in RStudio.

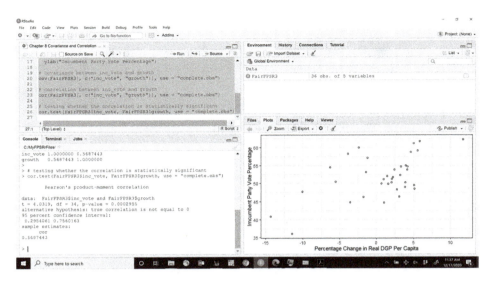

Figure 8.5 Output from cor.test command

8.5   EXERCISES

1. Open the script file named "Chapter 8 Tabular Analysis Example.R" in RStudio. Make sure that you have the correct directory path for loading the data. In other words, if "C:\MyFPSRrFiles" is not where you have your data, change this part of the script file so that the data load into RStudio. Once you have done this, run the code to produce the example output presented in Section 8.2 of this book.

    (a) Calculate a chi-squared test for the output presented in Figure 8.1. Report the results of this test and write about what it tells you about the theory that voters in union households are more likely to support candidates from the left.

    (b) A commonly expressed theory of politics is that people who are dissatisfied with the performance of the legislature are more likely to vote for candidates who are political outsiders. Test this theory with a hypothesis test using the variables "StronglyDisapproveCongress" (coded as "1" if the respondent reported that they strongly disapprove of the way that Congress was doing its job) and "V2Trump." Produce an appropriate table to show what you have found and report the results from a chi-squared test for the hypothesis test. Write about what this analysis tells you about the theory in question.

2. Open the script file named "Chapter 8 Difference of Means Example.R" in RStudio. Make sure that you have the correct directory path for loading the data. In other words, if "C:\MyFPSRrFiles" is not where you have your data, change this part of the script file so that the data load into RStudio.

    (a) Once you have done this, run the code to produce Figures 8.1 and 8.2 from *FPSR*. Copy and paste these figures into your word processing document.

(b)   A commonly expressed theory of politics is that governments which contain the party which got the most votes at the last election have more of an electoral mandate and thus will last longer. Test this theory with a hypothesis test using the variables "eptyplur" (coded as "1" if the party which received the most votes was in the government and "0" otherwise) and "govttime." Produce appropriate figures and a table to show what you have found and report the results from a t-test for the hypothesis test. Write about what this analysis tells you about the theory in question.

3.   Open the script file named "Chapter 8 Covariance and Correlation Example.R" in RStudio. Make sure that you have the correct directory path for loading the data. In other words, if "C:\MyFPSRrFiles" is not where you have your data, change this part of the script file so that the data load into RStudio.

(a)   Once you have done this, run the code to produce Figure 8.3 from *FPSR*. Copy and paste this figure into your word processing document.

(b)   As we discuss in *FPSR*, there are many different ways to measure economic performance, the independent variable in the theory of economic voting. Go through the steps that we go through in the lab but replace the variable "growth" with "inflation." Produce an appropriate figure and a table to show what you have found and report the results from a t-test for the hypothesis test on the correlation coefficient. Write about what this analysis tells you about the theory of economic voting.

9 TWO-VARIABLE REGRESSION MODELS

9.1 OVERVIEW

In Chapter 9 of *FPSR* we introduce the two-variable regression model. As we discuss, this is another two-variable hypothesis test that amounts to fitting a line through a scatterplot of observations on a dependent variable and an independent variable. In this chapter, we walk you through how to estimate such a bivariate model in R using RStudio.

9.2 ESTIMATING A TWO-VARIABLE REGRESSION

The estimation of a two-variable regression model, as discussed in Chapter 9 of *FPSR*, is fairly straightforward. The syntax is

ModelName = lm(*DependentVariable* ~*IndependentVariable*, data = *DataSet*)

where "*ModelName*" is the name you give to your model, "lm" is the command which tells R to estimate a regression model, "*DependentVariable*" is the name of the dependent variable, "*IndependentVariable*" is the name of the independent variable, and "*DataSet*" is the name of the data set, which must be loaded into RStudio, on which we want to estimate the regression model.

So, to estimate the model of incumbent vote as a function of economic growth that we feature so prominently in Chapter 9 of *FPSR*, you would submit the following command:

```
model = lm(inc_vote ~growth, data = FairFPSR3)
```

Figure 9.1 shows what RStudio looks like after this command has been successfully submitted. This is very different from what we would expect to see if we were estimating a regression model in most other statistical software programs. In most programs, we would expect to see a bunch of numerical output like what we see in Figure 9.5 of *FPSR*. One thing that you might have noticed that is in Figure 9.1 is a data element named "model" under the "Environment" tab in the upper-right part of the RStudio window.

In order to produce output such as that pictured in Figure 9.5 of *FPSR*, we need to

run a summary command, in this case,

summary(model)

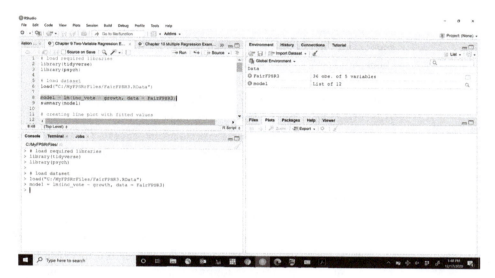

Figure 9.1 RStudio after the estimation of a two-variable regression model

Figure 9.2 Model summary output for a two-variable regression

which tells R to present output from the model. The output from this model is now displayed in the console window in the lower-left part of Figure 9.2.

9.3   GRAPHING A TWO-VARIABLE REGRESSION

To better understand what is going on in a two-variable regression model, it is often helpful to graph the regression line. An example of this is presented in Figure 9.4 of

FPSR. The code for producing a figure very similar to this in R is

```
FairFPSR3 %>%
mutate(fitted = as.numeric(fitted(model))) %>%
ggplot(aes(x=growth)) +
geom_point(aes(y = inc_vote) )+
geom_line( aes(y=fitted, group=1,)) +
theme_bw() +
theme(legend.title=element_blank()) +
xlab("Percentge Change in Real DGP per capita") +
ylab("Incumbent Party Vote Percentage") +
geom_hline(yintercept=mean(FairFPSR3$inc_vote), linetype="dashed") +
geom_vline(xintercept=mean(FairFPSR3$growth), linetype="dashed")
```

9.4   EXERCISES

1. Open the script file named "Chapter 9 Two-Variable Regression Examples.R" in RStudio. Make sure that you have the correct directory path for loading the data. In other words, if "C:\MyFPSRrFiles" is not where you have your data, change this part of the script file so that the data load into RStudio. Once you have done this, run the code to produce Figure 9.4 from *FPSR.* Copy and paste this figure into your word processing document.

2. If we change the independent variable from our running example from growth to inflation, what would the theory of economic voting lead us to expect in terms of a hypothesis for the slope of a regression line with variable inc_vote as the dependent variable and inflation as the independent variable? Explain your answer.

3. Estimate a regression model with the variable inc_vote as the dependent variable and inflation as the independent variable.

    (a) Copy and paste this output into your word processing document.

    (b) Write about the results from the hypothesis test that you discussed above. What does this tell you about the theory of economic voting?

    (c) Produce a figure like Figure 9.4 from *FPSR* but with inflation as the independent variable (inc_vote should remain as the dependent variable). Copy and paste this figure into your word processing document.

10 MULTIPLE REGRESSION: THE BASICS

10.1 OVERVIEW

In Chapter 10 of *FPSR*, we introduce the multiple regression model in which we are able to estimate the effect of X on Y holding Z constant. Here, we show you how to execute such models in R.

10.2 ESTIMATING A MULTIPLE REGRESSION

The estimation of a multiple regression model, as discussed in Chapters 10 and 11 of *FPSR*, is just an extension of the command used for estimating a two-variable regression. For example, if we have three independent variables, the syntax is

ModelName = lm(*DependentVariable* ~*IndependentVariable1* +
IndependentVariable2 + *IndependentVariable3*, data = *DataSet*)

where "*DependentVariable*" is the name of the dependent variable, and the terms that begin with "*IndependentVariable*" are the names of the independent variables.[1] For R's multiple regression command, the name of the dependent variable must always come first, followed by the names of the independent variables after the ~. The order in which the independent variables appear does not matter; you will get the same results regardless of their order.

The commands to estimate the multiple regression displayed under the column titled "C" in Table 10.1 of *FPSR* and to display the results from it are

```
model5 = lm(inc_vote ~growth + goodnews,
data = subset(FairFPSR3, FairFPSR3$year>1945))
summary(model5)
```

And we can produce the output from this which produces output like that displayed in Figure 10.1.

---

[1] In this example of the syntax, we have chosen to show the syntax for having three independent variables. In practice, you may have as many independent variables as you want in a regression model as long as you meet the minimum mathematical requirements that each independent variable varies, $n > k$, and you have no perfect multicollinearity. The first two of these requirements are discussed in Section 9.5 and the third is discussed in Section 10.7 of *FPSR*.

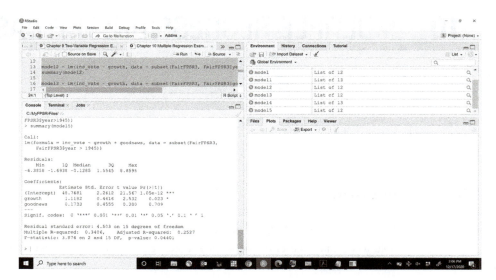

Figure 10.1 Basic output from a multiple regression

10.3   FROM REGRESSION OUTPUT TO TABLE – MAKING ONLY ONE TYPE OF COMPARISON

As we discuss in Section 10.9 of *FPSR*, when presenting the results from more than two regression models in the same table, it is important that we set up our comparisons appropriately – either as comparisons of different model specifications estimated with the same sample of data, or the same model specification estimated with different samples of data. This is because if both the sample of data and the model specification change, then we can not know for sure whether any differences in the estimates that we are observing are due to the different sample or the different specification.

10.3.1   Comparing Models with the Same Sample of Data, but Different Specifications

If your data set doesn't have any missing values for any of the variables that you want to include in a set of models with different specifications, then making a table for such comparisons is pretty straightforward. All that you need to do is to estimate the regressions of interest to you and put them into separate columns of a table. If, as is often the case, you have some missing values for some of the variables that you are including in your different models, then you need to take some extra steps in order to make sure that the regressions that you are comparing are all estimated with the exact same observations.

As an example of this, we will use the regressions that were used to produce the results presented in Table 10.1 of *FPSR*. If you compare the output presented in Figure 10.1 with that presented in Figure 9.5 of *FPSR*, one thing that you might notice is that the regression presented in Figure 9.5 of *FPSR* has 36 observations, whereas the regression presented in Figure 10.1 has 35. This is the case because the variable goodnews is missing for the 1876 election. Thus to obtain the output presented in

Table 10.1 of *FPSR*, it is necessary to exclude the observation for 1876 from the model that we estimate to produce the results presented in Column "**A**" of Table 10.1 of *FPSR*. One way to do this, given that we know the year of the observation that we want to exclude would be to write the command as

```
model2 = lm(inc_vote ~growth,
data = subset(FairFPSR3, FairFPSR3$year!=1876))
```

which tells R to estimate a regression with `inc_vote` as the dependent variable and `growth` as the independent variable using *only* that "subset" of observations for which the variable year is not equal to 1876 ("`year!=1876`" where "`!=`" means "is not equal to").

But what would we do if we didn't know exactly which observations are missing particular values of particular independent variables?[2] One of the easiest ways is just to estimate the model using all cases that are not missing for any of the independent variables that you plan to include in the models that you want to present. In our running example, we would estimate the following two models:

```
model3 = lm(inc_vote ~growth,
data = subset(FairFPSR3, FairFPSR3$goodnews!=1876|is.na(FairFPSR3$goodnews)))

model4 = lm(inc_vote ~goodnews,
data = subset(FairFPSR3, FairFPSR3$growth!=1876))
```

which would create the output presented in Table 10.1 of *FPSR*.

10.3.2   Comparing Models with the Same Specification, but Different Samples of Data

As an example of how to compare models with the same specification, but different samples of data, let's imagine that we want to look at the results from our running example of economic voting in the United States for the observations after World War II compared with all observations before then. Although there are some different interpretations of when the war started, most people agree that World War II ended in 1945. So, to estimate models on samples of data after the war and all other cases, we would estimate the following two models:

```
model5 = lm(inc_vote ~growth + goodnews,
data = subset(FairFPSR3, FairFPSR3$year>1945))

model6 = lm(inc_vote ~growth + goodnews,
data = subset(FairFPSR3, FairFPSR3$year<1945))
```

where the commands are identical except for the conditions written after the "subset."

---

[2] If an observation is missing for the dependent variable, it will not be included in any of the models that we estimate. Also, in general, we should have gotten to know our data before we estimate a regression model, and part of getting to know one's data is figuring out what are the missing values and why they are missing.

10.4   STANDARDIZED COEFFICIENTS

In order to obtain standardized coefficients, as discussed in Section 10.5 of *FPSR*, we would first estimate the model normally:

```
model1 = lm(inc_vote ~growth + goodnews, data = FairFPSR3)
```

and then run the command

```
lm.beta(model1)
```

which will produce the output displayed in Figure 10.2.

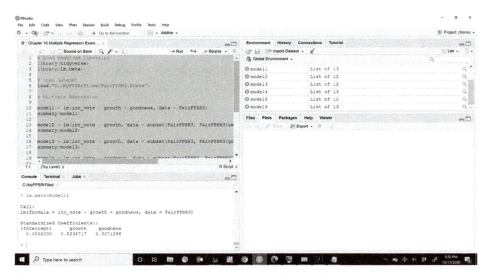

Figure 10.2   Basic output from a multiple regression with the "beta" coefficients

10.5   EXERCISES

1.   Open the script file named "Chapter 10 Multiple Regression Examples.R" in RStudio. Make sure that you have the correct directory path for loading the data. In other words, if "C:\MyFPSRrFiles" is not where you have your data, change this part of the script file so that the data load into RStudio. Once you have done this, run the code to produce the output shown in Figure 10.1. Copy and paste this figure into your word processing document.

2.   Estimate a multiple regression model with both inflation and growth as the independent variables and inc_vote as the dependent variable. Estimate the two two-variable models needed to make a table like Table 10.1 of *FPSR* where you are comparing the results across three specifications on the same sample of observations. Put your results into a table in your word processing document and write about what you have found.

3.   Estimate the two multiple regression models described in this chapter with the same specification but where the sample is divided according to whether the

observation occurred before or after 1945. Put these results into a table in your word processing document and write about what you have found.

4. Estimate a multiple regression model with standardized coefficients with good-news, inflation, and growth as the independent variables and inc_vote as the dependent variable. Put your results into a table in your word processing document and write about what you have found.

11 MULTIPLE REGRESSION MODEL SPECIFICATION

11.1 OVERVIEW

In Chapter 11 of *FPSR* we discuss a series of issues that researchers commonly encounter when they are trying to test their theories using multiple regression models. The advice for how to proceed when one encounters these issues involves a series of additional commands in R, which we detail in this chapter.

11.2 DUMMY VARIABLES

As we discuss in Section 11.2 of *FPSR*, dummy variables are variables that take on one of two different values. The vast majority of the time in political science, these two values are "zero" and "one." Dummy variables are usually created and named so that "one" represents the presence of a condition and "zero" represents the absence of that condition. In order not to confuse the people who will be reading your work or watching your presentations, it is a good idea to follow these conventions. For example, if you have a dummy variable to identify the gender identity of a survey respondent, it might be tempting to call the variable "gender." That, however, would leave unclear the issue of what the zeros and ones represent. If, by contrast, you named your variable "female," then the convention would be that a zero is for male respondents – or the absence of the condition "female" – and one is for the female respondents – the presence of the condition "female."

11.2.1 Creating New Variables

Sometimes data sets that you are working with come with all of the variables that you need already created for you. When they do not, you will need to create your own variables. Here is one large command in which we rename several variables and create a new dummy variable:

```
ANES1996small = ANES1996small %>%
rename(hillary_thermo = v960281,
income = v960701,
womenmvmt_thermo = v961039) %>%
mutate(female = ifelse(v960066==1, 0, 1),
womenmvmt_thermo_female=womenmvmt_thermo*female)
```

which tells R on the first line to start with the data set "ANES1996small," which is a subset of the 1996 American National Election Study. The second, third, and fourth lines tell R to rename the variables "v960281" and "v960701" with names that are more communicative about what each variable measures. On the fifth line, we create a new dummy variable using a combination of "mutate" and "ifelse." From the codebook for "ANES1996small," we can tell that the coding of values for each respondent's self-identified gender is in the variable named "V90066" and that the values of this variable are equal to 1 for "male" and 2 for "female." As we discuss in Section 11.2 of *FPSR*, we generally like our dummy variables to equal either one or zero and to have names that tell us about how the variable is coded. As we've seen before, "mutate" tells R that we are going to change something. The "ifelse" statement is a function that tells R to test a logical argument and, if it is true, to do one thing and, if the logical argument is not true, to do something else. So this line of code tells R to create a new variable named "female" and, if v960066 is equal to one, to make female equal to zero, and otherwise to make it equal to one. Finally, on the sixth line of this command, we create a new variable named "womenmvmt_thermo_female" that is the product of "womenmvmt_thermo" times "female," the variable that we use in our example of interactions.

Whenever you create a new variable, it is critically important to check that you created exactly what you intended to create. One way to check this is with a CrossTable command which we introduced in Chapter 8 of this volume. In this case, we could check our work with the command:

```
CrossTable(ANES1996small$v960066, ANES1996small$female)
```

which tells R to create a two-variable table with the values of v960066 and female. From the results in the console window of Figure 11.1, we can see that we did create the variable that we wanted.

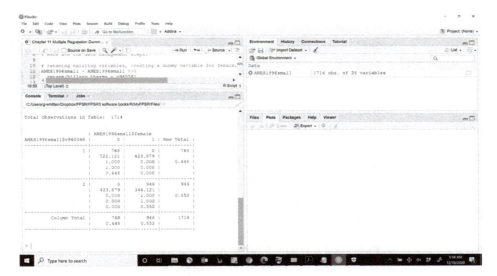

Figure 11.1 Output from checking whether we correctly coded the dummy variable female

Figure 11.2 Output from a regression model with a dummy variable

11.2.2   Estimating a Multiple Regression Model with a Single Dummy Independent Variable

As we discussed in Chapter 10 of this software book, the syntax for estimating a multiple regression with three independent variables is:

$ModelName$ = lm($DependentVariable$ ~$IndependentVariable1$ + $IndependentVariable2$ + $IndependentVariable3$, data = $DataSet$)

where "$DependentVariable$" is the name of the dependent variable, and the "$IndependentVariable$" terms are the names of the three independent variables. When we have only a single dummy independent variable, then we just simply add the name of that variable to the list after the "~".

As an example of this, we can estimate the regression model displayed on the left side of Table 11.1 of *FPSR* with the following command:

```
model1 = lm(hillary_thermo ~income + female, data = ANES1996small)
```

where "hillary_thermo" is the dependent variable, respondents' thermometer ratings of Hillary Clinton, "income" is a continuous independent variable, and "female" is the dummy independent variable that we just created. Note that, as was the case with our multiple regression models with multiple continuous independent variables, the order of the independent variables does not matter for this command. The output from this model is displayed in Figure 11.2.

11.2.3   Estimating a Multiple Regression Model with Multiple Dummy Independent Variables

To estimate a multiple regression model with multiple dummy variables, you use the same command syntax as in the previous section. The main complication comes when the multiple dummy variables represent values for a categorical variable with more than two values. As we discuss in Section 11.2.2 of *FPSR*, in such a case, in order to avoid what is known as the "dummy variable trap," you need to leave one category of such an independent variable out of the regression model, and that left out category becomes the "reference category."

11.3 DUMMY VARIABLES IN INTERACTIONS

In Section 11.3 of *FPSR*, we discuss testing interactive hypotheses with dummy variables. There are several different ways to do this in R. We recommend that you use a fairly straightforward approach in which the first step is to create a new variable that is the product of the two variables in the interaction as we did in Section 11.2.1. We can then run the following two commands to produce the desired regression output:

```
model2=lm(hillary_thermo~womenmvmt_thermo+female+womenmvmt_thermo_female,
data = ANES1996small)
summary(model2)
```

The output from this command is displayed in Figure 11.3.

Figure 11.3 Output from a regression model with an interaction

11.4 POST-ESTIMATION DIAGNOSTICS IN R FOR OLS

In Chapter 11 of *FPSR* we discuss a number of diagnostic procedures that can be carried out once an OLS model has been estimated. These procedures are all available in R.

11.4.1 Identifying Outliers and Influential Cases in OLS

Figure 11.4 in *FPSR* shows the results from an lvr2plot which is short for "leverage-versus-residual-squared plot" and is a standard plot in Stata. As far as we know, R does

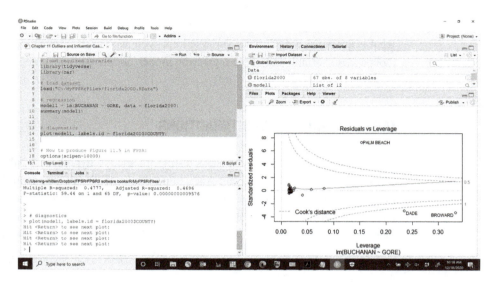

Figure 11.4 Output from a regression model with an interaction

not have syntax for creating a plot *exactly* like this. The closest command that we know of for producing a figure that lets us see similar information in R is the following:

```
plot(model1, labels.id = florida2000$COUNTY)
```

which produces four different diagnostic plots. To see them after having run this command, you need to click on the console window in the lower-left and hit return until you get to the last plot. Figure 11.4 shows what you will see once you do this.

At first glance, the plot in the lower-right corner of Figure 11.4 looks very different from Figure 11.4 in *FPSR*, but it does contain the same basic information. The first major difference is that the vertical and horizontal axes are reversed: in the R plot, leverage is the horizontal axis, whereas in Figure 11.4 in *FPSR*, leverage is the vertical axis. Otherwise, the measure of leverage is identical across the two figures. To see this, look at the leverage values for Broward and Dade counties in each plot – they are identical. The second major difference is that the Stata lvr2plot displays squared normalized residuals whereas the "Residuals vs Leverage" plot from R displays standardized residuals.[1] This means that in the Stata plot, relatively large residuals will always be located to the right in lvr2plots. In contrast, in the R Residuals versus Leverage plot, relatively large residuals will be nearer to either the top or the bottom of the plots. So, for instance, we know that Palm Beach county had a relatively large positive residual value whereas Broward and Dade counties had relative large negative residual values. Thus, in the lvr2plot, where residual values are squared, all three will be towards the right side of the plot relative to the residuals for the other counties. And, in the Residuals vs Leverage

---

[1] The "normalization" or "standardization" of values is a minor technical detail. In both cases, it means that the residual values are not in the same metric as the dependent variable. But, because what we care about are relative comparisons between the *relative* magnitude of the residuals across cases, the exact details of how these measures were standardized or normalized is not a concern.

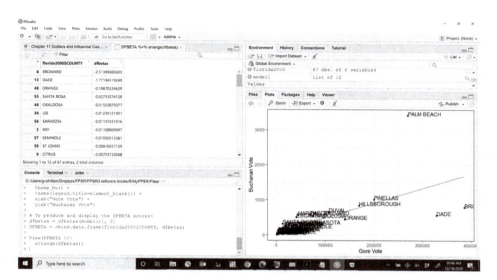

Figure 11.5 Examining DFBETA values

plot, the Palm Beach residual will be near the top of the plot while that for Broward and Dade counties will be near the bottom. In terms of the bottom line conclusion, both plots lead us to the same place – Broward, Dade, and Palm Beach all had a large influence on the model.

Table 11.8 in *FPSR* shows the five largest DFBETA scores from a regression model. The commands for estimating DFBETA scores and viewing them in R using this example are the following:

```
dfbetas = dfbetas(model1)[, 2]
DFBETA = cbind.data.frame(florida2000$COUNTY, dfbetas)
View(DFBETA %>%
arrange(dfbetas))
```

As we can see in Figure 11.5, this pops open a new data set in which the DFBETA scores are sorted from smallest to largest, with Broward and Dade at the top of the data set and Palm Beach at the bottom.

Detecting Multicollinearity in OLS

As we discussed in Section 11.5 of *FPSR*, one way to detect multicollinearity is to estimate a Variance Inflation Factor (or "VIF") for each independent variable after you have estimated your regression model. The syntax for producing this type of figure in R is:

```
vif(ModelName)
```

where "*ModelName*" is the name of the model for which you want the VIF calculations. To see an example of how we do this, we can estimate the regression that produces "Model 3" in Table 11.2 of *FPSR* with the following command:

```
model1 = lm(bush_therm ~income + ideology + education + partyid,
data = nes2004subset)
```

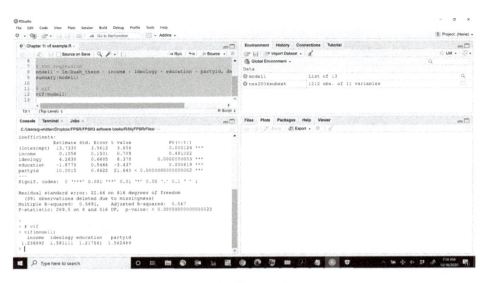

Figure 11.6 Output from a regression model and a vif command

And then run the following command:

`vif(model1)`

which will produce the output which is displayed in Figure 11.6.

11.5   EXERCISES

1.   Open the script file named "Chapter 11 Multiple Regression Dummy Variable Examples.R" in RStudio. Make sure that you have the correct directory path for loading the data. In other words, if "C:\MyFPSRrFiles" is not where you have your data, change this part of the script file so that the data load into RStudio. Once you have done this, run the code to produce the output shown in Figure 11.2. Copy and paste this into your word processing document.

2.   Run the code to produce the output shown in Figure 11.3. Copy and paste this into your word processing document.

3.   Create a dummy variable identifying male respondents. Estimate the model displayed in Figure 11.2 with this new variable instead of the variable identifying female respondents. Copy and paste this into your word processing document. Write a brief summary of what these results tell you.

4.   Create an interaction between the new dummy variables that you created to identify male respondents and the women's movement thermometer. Estimate the model displayed in Figure 11.3 with this new variable instead of the variables identifying female respondents. Copy and paste this into your word processing document. Write a brief summary of what these results tell you.

5.   Open the script file named "Chapter 11 Outliers and Influential Cases Examples.R" in RStudio. Once you have done this and made sure that you have the correct data set loaded into R, run the regression with votes for Buchanan as the

dependent variable and votes for Gore as the independent variable. Copy and paste this output into your word processing document.

6.   Run the code to produce the plot that is displayed in Figure 11.4. Copy and paste this figure into your word processing document.

7.   Run the code to produce Figure 11.5 of *FPSR*. Copy and paste this figure into your word processing document.

8.   Run the code to produce the DFBETA scores that are presented in Table 11.8 of *FPSR*. In your word processing document, list the DFBETA values for the five counties with the smallest (in absolute values) scores for this calculation together with their DFBETA scores.

9.   Open the script file named "Chapter 11 vif example.R." Once you have done this and made sure that you have the correct data set loaded into RStudio, run the regression model and the vif command. Copy and paste this output into your word processing document.

12 LIMITED DEPENDENT VARIABLES AND TIME-SERIES DATA

12.1 OVERVIEW

In Chapter 12 of *FPSR* we discuss two important extensions to multiple regression models; models with dichotomous dependent variables and models with time-series data. In this chapter we provide an explanation of the commands needed to deal with these circumstances in R.

12.2 MODELS WITH DUMMY DEPENDENT VARIABLES

As we discuss in Chapter 12 of *FPSR*, there are several different models that can be used when we have a dummy dependent variable. In this set of examples, we will work with data from the 2004 American National Election Study (ANES) with a dependent variable named "Bush," which equals one for respondents who reported that they voted for George W. Bush and equals zero for those respondents who reported that they voted for John Kerry.[1] To get a look at the values for this variable, we can run a `CrossTable` command

```
CrossTable(nes2004subset$bush)
```

which produces the output displayed in Figure 12.1. As we discuss in Chapter 12 of *FPSR*, one option when we have a limited dependent variable is simply to estimate a regression model using the standard syntax that we discussed in Chapter 10 of this book. For example, if we have three independent variables, the command is

ModelName = lm(*DependentVariable* ~*IndependentVariable1* + *IndependentVariable2* + *IndependentVariable3*, data = *DataSet*)

and the only difference is that the *DependentVariable* is a dummy variable. So, if we want to estimate the model displayed in Table 12.1 of *FPSR*, we would write the command as

```
model_LPM = lm(bush ~partyid + eval_WoT + eval_HoE, data = nes2004subset)
```

---

[1] This is the same example that we use in Chapter 12 of *FPSR*. For a more detailed explanation of the variable and how it was created, see footnote 1 on page 274 of *FPSR*.

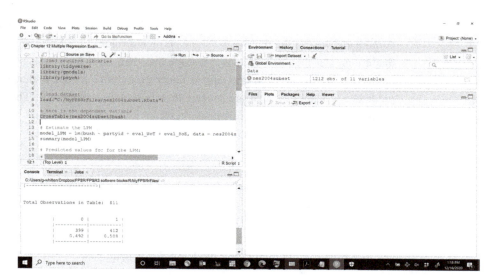

Figure 12.1 Table of values for the variable "Bush"

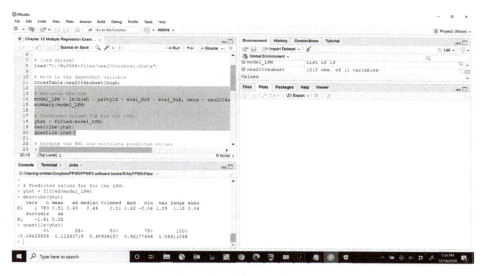

Figure 12.2 Calculating and displaying the predicted values from the linear probability model

where "bush" is the dependent variable for which the values are displayed in Figure 12.1, "partyid" is "Party Identification," "eval_WoT" is "Evaluation: War on Terror," and "eval_HoE" is "Evaluation: Health of the Economy." To calculate and summarize the predicted probabilities from this model, we use the following commands with what should now be familiar syntax

```
yhat = fitted(model_LPM)
describe(yhat)
quantile(yhat)
```

which produces the output displayed in Figure 12.2. If we look at the results from these commands, we can see that we get some predicted values (what we refer to as $\hat{P}_i$ values) that are greater than one and some that are less than zero. As we discuss in Chapter 12 of *FPSR*, one of the problems of the linear probability model is that it can produce predicted probabilities that are greater than one or less than zero. This is one of the main reasons why political scientists prefer to use either a binomial logit model or a binomial probit model when they have a dummy dependent variable.

To estimate a binomial logit model in R, the syntax is

```
ModelName = glm(DependentVariable ~ IndependentVariable1 +
IndependentVariable2 + IndependentVariable3, data = DataSet, family =
binomial(link = "logit"))
```

and to estimate a binomial probit model in R, the syntax is

```
ModelName = glm(DependentVariable ~ IndependentVariable1 +
IndependentVariable2 + IndependentVariable3, data = DataSet, family =
binomial(link = "probit"))
```

As we discuss in Chapter 12 of *FPSR*, with each of these types of models there is an estimated systematic component for each observation, what we call the $X_i\hat{\beta}$ values, that can be put through a link function to produce predicted probabilities, what we refer to as $\hat{P}_i$ values. The command for calculating the $\hat{P}_i$ values after either a binomial logit or binomial probit has been estimated is

```
newvariable=fitted(ModelName)
```

where "`newvariable`" is the name of the new variable that we want to create, and the "`fitted`" tells R that we want the new variable to be the predicted probabilities for each of our observations that was included in the model estimation.

So, to continue with our running example, we can produce the logit and probit columns of the results displayed in Table 12.2 of *FPSR* and predicted probabilities for each observation by running the following lines of code

```
model_BNL=glm(bush~partyid+eval_WoT+eval_HoE, data=nes2004subset,
family = binomial(link = "logit"))
summary(model_BNL)
p_BNL = fitted(model_BNL)

model_BNP=glm(bush partyid+eval_WoT+eval_HoE, data=nes2004subset,
family = binomial(link = "probit"))
summary(model_BNP)
p_BNP = fitted(model_BNP)
```

We can then display summary statistics for the resulting predicted probabilities by running the following lines of code

```
describe(p_BNL)
quantile(p_BNL)
describe(p_BNP)
quantile(p_BNP)
```

which produces the output presented in Figure 12.3.

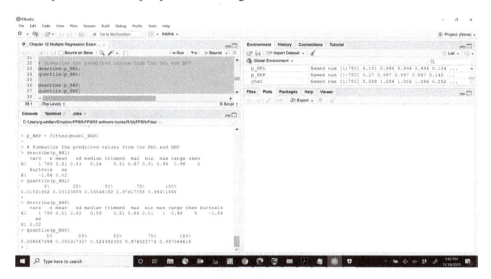

Figure 12.3 Summary statistics for predicted values from a binomial logit model and a binomial probit model

In order to produce classification tables like Table 12.3 in *FPSR*, we need first to create a new variable which is the predicted value of the dependent variable, what we have labeled "Model-based expectations" in Table 12.3. For the linear probability model in this example, we would use the following six lines of code

```
nes2004subset_2 = nes2004subset %>%
select(bush, partyid, eval_WoT, eval_HoE) %>%
drop_na() %>%
mutate(p_vote_lpm = ifelse(yhat>0.5, 1, 0),
p_vote_bnl = ifelse(p_BNL>0.5, 1, 0),
p_vote_bnp = ifelse(p_BNP>0.5, 1, 0))
```

where we first create a new variable `p_vote_lpm` equal to the predicted values from the linear probability model that we estimated. We then recode the values of `p_vote_lpm` so that predicted probabilities of 0.5 or smaller become predictions that the individual will vote for Kerry (coded as zero) and predicted probabilities greater than 0.5 become predictions that the individual will vote for Bush (coded as one). We then produce a table of the values of actual vote and our model-based predictions. The output from these commands is presented in Figure 12.4.

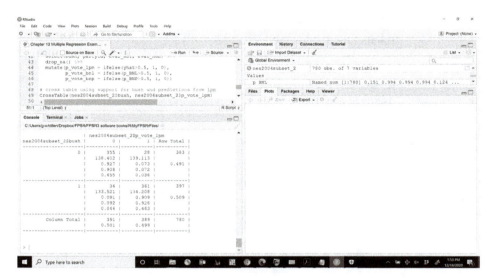

Figure 12.4 Raw output used to produce Table 12.3 of *FPSR*

12.3   EXERCISES

1.   Open the script file named "Chapter 12 Multiple Regression Examples.R" in RStudio. Make sure that you have the correct directory path for loading the data. In other words, if "C:\MyFPSRrFiles" is not where you have your data, change this part of the script file so that the data load into RStudio. Once you have done this, run the code to produce the results presented in Table 12.2 of *FPSR*. Copy and paste this figure into your word processing document.

2.   Using the code at the bottom of "Chapter 12 Multiple Regression Examples.R" create a classification table for the BNL and the BNP models. Copy and paste this into your word processing document.

3.   Calculate the proportionate reduction in error from a naive model to the BNL and from a naive model to the BNP. Write briefly about what you have learned from doing this.

BIBLIOGRAPHY

Bansak, Kirk, Jens Hainmueller, & Dominik Hangartner. 2016. "How economic, humanitarian, and religious concerns shape European attitudes toward asylum seekers." *Science* 354(6309): 217–222.

De Mesquita, Bruce Bueno, James D. Morrow, Randolph M. Siverson, & Alastair Smith. 1999. "An institutional explanation of the democratic peace." *American Political Science Review* 93(4):791–807.

Fair, Ray C. 1978. "The effect of economic events on votes for president." *The Review of Economics and Statistics* 60:159–173.

Fortunato, David, Randolph T. Stevenson, & Greg Vonnahme. 2016. "Context and political knowledge: Explaining cross-national variation in partisan left-right knowledge." *The Journal of Politics* 78(4):1211–1228.

Heberlig, Eric, Marc Hetherington, & Bruce Larson. 2006. "The price of leadership: Campaign money and the polarization of congressional parties." *The Journal of Politics* 68(4):992–1005.

King, Gary, Benjamin Schneer, & Ariel White. 2017. "How the news media activate public expression and influence national agendas." *Science* 358(6364):776–780.

Lipsmeyer, Christine S. & Heather Nicole Pierce. 2011. "The eyes that bind: Junior ministers as oversight mechanisms in coalition governments." *The Journal of Politics* 73(4):1152–1164.

O'Brien, Diana Z. 2015. "Rising to the top: Gender, political performance, and party leadership in parliamentary democracies." *American Journal of Political Science* 59(4):1022–1039.

Stasavage, David. 2005. "Democracy and education spending in Africa." *American Journal of Political Science* 49(2):343–358.

Titiunik, Rocio. 2016. "Drawing your senator from a jar: Term length and legislative behavior." *Political Science Research and Methods* 4(2):293–316.

INDEX

R commands and syntax are emboldened.